Looking for More?

"There must be more to a relationship than this" . . . deep down you crave that psychic touch of a soulmate—that special relationship that goes beyond your normal relationships into a far different quality of being. When you find your soulmate, the feeling will be completely different; it is so profound, so intimate, so right—and so inevitable!

If you're reading this now, you have at least a curiosity, if not a craving, to complement yourself. That's a desire of many people.

You're probably asking one or more of the many questions that people ask Arian Sarris all the time: How do you find your soulmate? Where are they? How do you know when you've met your soulmate? When you meet them, does it mean you always get to be together? What happens when they die? Why haven't we found each other? Suppose you missed them? What if they died young? Or got involved with someone else? What's the problem? It is me?

Those questions are neither inane or trivial, and this book will answer all of them plus give you step-by-step guidance in preparing for and locating your soulmate.

About the Author

Arian Sarris is a licensed transpersonal marriage and family therapist and a long-time practicing psychic and conscious channel. She has taught many seminars, workshops, and classes in North America and Europe, and currently has a practice in northern California, where her combination of psychic and psychotherapeutic skills help clients experience deep, tangible, and long-lasting change within both their personal and spiritual dimensions. She is also the author of *Healing the Past* (Llewellyn, 1997).

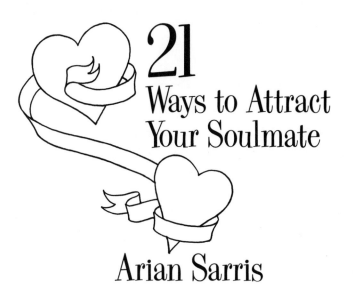

21
Ways to Attract
Your Soulmate

Arian Sarris

2000
Llewellyn Publications
St. Paul, Minnesota 55164-0383, U.S.A.

First Edition
Second Printing, 2000

Book design and editing by Rebecca Zins
Cover design and chapter opener illustration by William Merlin Cannon
Interior illustrations by Carrie Westfall

Library of Congress Cataloging-in-Publication Data
Sarris, Arian, 1946-
   21 ways to attract your soulmate / Arian Sarris.
      p.   cm.
   ISBN 1-56718-611-4
   1. Soul mates.   I. Title: Twenty one ways to attract your soulmate.
      II. Title.
BF1045.I58 S37 2000
646.7'7—dc21   99-048187

Llewellyn Publications
A Division of Llewellyn Worldwide, Ltd.
P.O. Box 64383, Dept. K611-4
St. Paul, MN 55164-0383, U.S.A.
www.llewellyn.com

 Printed in the United States of America on recycled paper

To Write to the Author

If you wish to contact the author or would like more information about this book, please write to the author in care of Llewellyn Worldwide and we will forward your request. Both the author and publisher appreciate hearing from you and learning of your enjoyment of this book and how it has helped you. Llewellyn Worldwide cannot guarantee that every letter written to the author can be answered, but all will be forwarded. Please write to:

Arian Sarris
℅ Llewellyn Worldwide
P.O. Box 64383, Dept. K611-4
St. Paul, MN 55164-0383, U.S.A.

Please enclose a self-addressed stamped envelope for reply, or $1.00 to cover costs. If outside U.S.A., enclose international postal reply coupon.

This book wouldn't have been conceived,
never mind written, if it weren't for
Leia Melead and Maynard Friesz.
And, of course, nothing would get done
without my dear friend Intz Walker.

Contents

The Exercises . . .

The Preparation

Soulmates

In the movie *Made in Heaven,* two souls meet in heaven and fall in love. They share a special magical bliss for awhile, and then the woman decides to incarnate on earth. Desperately unhappy at losing her, the man incarnates as well, hoping to find her again. Once embodied, he forgets his quest, even though they have several near-misses over the years. Finally, one day, as they are walking down the street, they sense something and turn. They see each other and fall into each other's arms. It's romantic, it's gooey. It's the soulmate connection in action!

No matter what kind of love relationship we have, good or bad, deep down we are craving the psychic touch of our soulmate—that special relationship that goes beyond our normal relationships into a far different quality of being. And we don't even know it until we experience it. No matter how we may express our desire to have a lover, when we find our soulmate, the feeling is completely different; it is so profound, so intimate, so right—and so inevitable!

How many of us have dreamed of this scenario: You happen to see a person across the room, and your eyes click together; you feel a jolt in your energy field that shudders through your whole being. You think, WOW! It's finally happened! You've met your soulmate at last! All our dreams have been fulfilled!

You have found your special partner—in love, in intimacy, in life.

Some people have described a soulmate as their other half, like identical twins born from one egg, so to speak, two parts of a whole, one soul in two bodies. When you come together, you experience that most intimate mind/being connection of completion and wholeness. There is nothing more profound than that shared bond. That's when you realize just what you've been missing for so long. This One Soulmate theory means you have only one opportunity for love because there's only that one special person.

Other people speak of multiple soulmates—not one exclusive partner, but a particular vibration that several soulmates share with you. These soulmates help you deal with the lessons, karma, or experiences that confront you during particular segments of your life. That means their time with you may vary; you may be lifelong mates, or you may drift apart after your work together is finished.

One of the implications of this kind of soulmate is that these relationships are affected by (and reflect) different levels of your personal development. Your soulmate in your twenties is surely far different from one in your forties because your attitudes, needs, and behaviors are different.

Nevertheless, their purpose for you (and yours for them) is to help you maneuver through the reefs of personal issues, fears, and needs and come through them safely and, hopefully, healthier.

I personally support the idea of multiple soulmates, each one having that essential soulmate vibration that you all share. (I inherently dislike the idea of "only one chance.") I also, however, believe that there is one very special person that you may or may not have been fortunate to meet—who is that other part of you. But whether it's your special essence partner, or just one of your vibrational soulmates, you deserve the experience of knowing the one who is right for you—who completes you—*at this time.*

The next step is to find them.

No matter what kind of soulmate you attract, of one thing you can be sure: they are familiar souls. You two have been together in other lives. Your experience with them was so potent, and your connection so strong, that you had no choice but to be with each other. It was like destiny. Since so many of us are very eager for self-development, self-healing, and personal growth, having these soulmate relationships will make our learning occur at a faster and more intense level.

If you're reading this book, you have at least a curiosity, if not a craving, to complete yourself. That's the desire of many people.

How do you find your soulmate? Where are they? How do you know when you've met your soulmate? When you meet them, does it mean you always get to be together? What happens when they die? Why haven't you two found each other? Suppose you missed them? What if they died young? Or got involved with someone else? What's the problem? Is it me? What's in the way? Is it my bad breath? My crooked teeth? My personality? (Those are judgments about yourself, not Truth.)

If you think those questions are inane or trivial, I guarantee they are not. People ask them all the time because they are afraid that they indeed have only one chance for true happiness, and since they aren't with their soulmate, they've missed their opportunity for this lifetime.

Having only one chance, only one opportunity—and once we miss that, it's gone—seems both unfair and illogical. To be unable to have a relationship with our soulmate, who shares so much with us and whose purpose is to help us both grow, means a whole part of our live's purpose may be thwarted—unless we intentionally decided before our births not to be together (and even that can be changed).

What's going on? What's keeping you two apart? There are all sorts of reasons, but I'll mention a few of them:

- Unfinished business with someone else

- Your unresolved family issues (big one!)

- No time, desire, or motivation

- Fear of getting what you really want

- Commitment issues

- Karma

These are some of the major reasons for being apart, although there are certainly others. But whatever they are, the result is still the same—you do not have a relationship with your soulmate.

Now you're doomed to search for them (consciously or unconsciously) everywhere. "Where's my soulmate?" you wonder, looking in the faces of everyone you meet, including the person you end up marrying or partnering with. You may ask them silently, "Are *you* my soulmate?"

You can't be sure because you don't know what your soulmate's energy feels like. How could you? You aren't familiar with it. So even if you *did* meet your soulmate, you might not even recognize them!

Then there's another scenario: You've met your soulmate, you've even had a relationship with them—and it's failed.

Aaron and Lisa announced, "We are soulmates." They got married; a few years later, when they broke up, Aaron declared, "That wasn't really my soulmate. I was mistaken." In fact, they were soulmates. If they believed in the one soulmate theory (which they did), the idea that their relationship had failed would have been too painful for them. They couldn't make it work. They'd never have another chance to be with their soulmate. (What a horrible thing to do to yourself!)

Denying that they were soulmates made the pain of the breakup more acceptable. Otherwise they would have been inundated with self-blame: "How could I have been so wrong? How could I have imagined Aaron/Lisa was my soulmate when they were obviously not!" By turning the relationship into a mistake, they are denying its reality in order to prevent self-blame and guilt from festering inside them.

When Aaron finally realized that there might be multiple soulmates, he could accept that he and Lisa were indeed soulmates, and that they had learned their lessons together. The relationship they created was right, *at that particular time,* for their personal development.

By taking the perspective that you two came together for a particular task or learning situation, it becomes easier for you to accept the lessons and move on.

Personally, I think the worst case scenario is being unable to activate *any* kind of relationship. And it happens all the time—because you're not ready to meet your soulmate.

What do you need to do to prepare for your soulmate? Lots of things. But they all require you to focus on yourself, to embrace your own change, and to trust in the process. As you do that, you begin to raise your own personal vibration to a higher level. That opens you up to new possibilities and attracts people who are looking for that new vibration.

It's like a radio. You can only receive whatever signals it is equipped to pick up. A shortwave radio gets more signals than a regular AM/FM radio, and a five-band radio receives many more signals. To increase your radio's range (i.e., expand its potential), you need to upgrade its innards or trade up to something with far more power and wider bandwidth.

What does that have to do with soulmates? If you're transmitting on AM and your soulmate is on FM, there won't be any connection between you. Or, if your AM/FM radio has a weak signal, it won't be able to receive many stations very well, one of which is your soulmate.

You need to pump up the juice. After all, you can't bring in your soulmate just by wishing. You need to light up like a Christmas tree, so the right person (and only that person) can see you. In fact, they won't be able to miss you!

How do you do that? By getting all your cells—your mind, your spirit, your heart, your being—*all* of you committed to the task of manifesting your soulmate.

There are many ways of doing that, as you will see when you browse through the upcoming exercises.

Committing

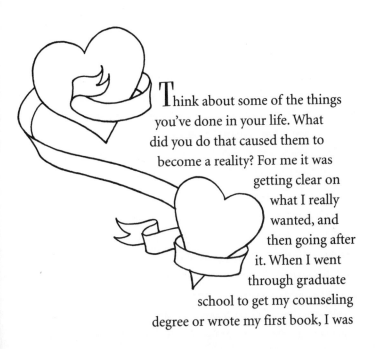

Think about some of the things you've done in your life. What did you do that caused them to become a reality? For me it was getting clear on what I really wanted, and then going after it. When I went through graduate school to get my counseling degree or wrote my first book, I was completely focused on those goals. Everything revolved around them.

But I wasn't always successful. I have many projects littered by the wayside, half done, vaguely begun, or merely doodles or ideas. There was something missing with them. They didn't catch fire inside me, they didn't get my full attention and focus. And I didn't commit to them one hundred percent in my being.

Meeting your soulmate is a project that requires one hundred percent commitment and focus. It's not enough to say, "Yes, I want to have that special relationship." You have to commit to creating a relationship with your soulmate even *before* they come to you. That's what this book is about—preparing you for your soulmate.

The ability to manifest your desires is directly connected to how well you focus your energy. Normally, we are very scatterbrained, so we need to learn how to focus. The more aligned we are in purpose and intent, the stronger our desire for our goal, the more powerful you become, and the more capable we become in manifesting what we want. So by focusing on manifesting your soulmate with all your heart and mind and body and spirit, nothing can stand in your way. You've become an irresistible force.

Then what?

There's a famous maxim: Be careful of what you ask for because you'll get it. If you're asking for your soulmate, you'll get them. The question to ask yourself is, are you ready for them? And are they ready for you?

As you work on bringing your soulmate into your life, many of your own expectations and desires will be exposed, giving you the opportunity to examine, alter, or even discard them, if necessary. They may include unreasonably high expectations, or ideas and feelings that don't bear any relation to the reality you want to manifest.

Fred told me, "I thought I met my soulmate, but she wasn't what I was hoping for, so I decided not to make the connection." How could he know without getting to know her better? His expectations and judgments were getting in the way.

Lesley's ideal man was six feet tall and muscular, and that's what she was scanning for. She, too, was looking for her expectations, not her reality. She found all sorts of men who fit her ideal, but none of them were her soulmate.

Only when you actually discard your expectations and start dreaming, imaging, and calling in your soulmate can you actually begin to sense the emotional, spiritual, and physical shape of that person. After Lesley did these exercises, she discovered that her soulmate was shorter than she was, which was a real shock; plus, he was sort of pudgy, which she wasn't happy about either. That forced her to confront her own attitudes around weight, good looks, perfection and the lack of it, which coincidentally were all tied up with her own self-esteem issues. Luckily, by the time she actually met him in person, she had already dealt with much of her anxiety and self-judgment. It turned out that he was neither as short nor as pudgy as she had feared (just an inch shorter, and about twenty pounds overweight)—but she could get past that and accept him because, most importantly, he was right for her.

How to Use This Book

Now that you've opened this book, your inclination may be to flip through the exercises, deciding which ones appeal to you and ignoring others that have no interest for you at all. That's because these ideas cover a wide range of possibilities. Some of them guide you to release old patterns, while others are aimed strictly at attraction.

You may feel a real temptation to do all of the attraction exercises and none of the release ones.

Resist that temptation!

If you don't do release work, the attraction exercises won't have the same power or impact. You need both release and attraction—release to let the old stuff go, and attraction to let in the new.

Other than that, there's no obligation to do all of the exercises. That's why there are twenty-one. Pick and choose the ones that feel right to you. (Refer to page 51, "Before You Start," for suggestions on the exercises that would be best for your level of commitment.) You also don't have to follow these exercises slavishly. If you find that you want to make a variation because you feel it adds more oomph or power to the experience, feel free to do so. They are not cast in concrete.

Since this is *your* mystical journey, you are being given the choice of different tools to help you in your work. By themselves, each one has its own strengths. As a group, they are incredibly powerful.

Every exercise strengthens your ability to magnetize your soulmate to you. After all, your soulmate may be out there trying to find you as well. They know they're not happy either, even if they have a relationship. That's what these exercises do—get you in vibrational sync with your soulmate.

Warnings

Relationships

If you find you're feeling guilty about doing this work because you're already in a relationship, *don't do this work.* You will manifest what you ask for. Then you're going to be in a real pickle. For goodness' sake, don't work on manifesting your soulmate if you're not prepared to have a relationship with them!

Overzealousness

Too many hours of work lead to burnout. Don't tackle fifteen exercises in a week. It will neither give you the benefit you want nor the kind of experience you're looking for. It's like jumping into a freezing pool: Your body will go into shock, which means you'll get sick or develop such a hostile reaction to the word "soulmate" that you'll run the other way!

Relax; take it slow. You just need a commitment to the process. Let it all unfold at its natural rhythm and pace.

Some of these exercises are designed to be done every day, like the chanting, affirmations/decrees, or the clean-out. Others take mindful preparation. Give yourself the time not only to do the work but to savor it, to feel its full benefit in your body and your energy field.

Free Will

Calling in your soulmate is an acceptable goal, but there is a caveat, and it's a big one: Free will. The other person can choose not to come, or not to stay.

These exercises do not let you take away their free will or violate their rights. It is their choice—and yours—whether you will become involved with each other. That is why we have free will.

If the relationship doesn't work out, here are some possible reasons:

- The connection was not meant to be

- You aren't ready for it yet

- You decided before you were born that you'd rather not meet in this lifetime

- There's stuff in the way that needs to be dealt with (karma) before you can join with each other

That's why all of this work must include the words *"in alignment with my highest good."* That doesn't mean what you *think* you want, but what your Higher Self *knows* is right for you. You might feel some pain now that things didn't work out, but in the future, you will be glad that mistakes weren't made.

My Caveat

Although I can make no promises about your finding your soulmate—after all, only you know whether you are ready—I guarantee one thing: You will change.

Cleaning the Closet

People often miss one very important piece of the relationship puzzle when they are trying to attract their soulmate. It's the part that says, "To let something new in, you have to release the old." Think of it as cleaning out your psychological closet by letting go of what's old, out-of-date, and useless. That means you need to clean out and release your fears, patterns, lovers, and family traditions that keep you stuck in the past in order to best prepare for your soulmate.

Imagine a clothes closet jammed full of clothes (for many of us that's pretty close to the mark). You can barely squeeze one more dress or suit or shirt into your closet, and you have to fight to pull them out, so they end up looking wrinkled and crushed. Many of them are gray, old, tired, torn, and out of style.

As a metaphor, it means that you're holding onto worn-out ideas, patterns, beliefs, desires, and fears, no matter how useless or outdated—just like your garments. It's time to examine them, air them out, and discard them, if necessary. That opens up space inside you to accept something new, at a higher level of development.

What does it take to change your inner patterns? It helps to actually start on the physical level by cleaning out a closet (if you don't want to tackle your clothes closet, try the attic, basement, garage, or kitchen). Spring cleaning, no matter what time of year it's done, allows you to sort through your clothes or other possessions and decide what you really want to keep and what it's time to let go of.

Allot yourself up to a whole day to clean out the closet. Believe it or not, it's a big project (not just physically, but emotionally). Letting go of your clothes, especially old favorites, can be quite traumatic.

As you sort through your clothes, consider the following questions or statements:

- Is this something I really want (or need) to wear? (Especially if it's tatty, gray, stained, old, dirty, and/or everyone's embarrassed to see you wearing it.)

- Is it something I really won't wear? (It's too big, too small, cut badly, doesn't hang right, makes me look like a moose.)

- Am I keeping it for its sentimental value, even though it's out of style? (But my first boyfriend loved me in that dress, even though it's a weird style and I can't fit in it now.)

- I've never worn it, but I liked it when I bought it; I may wear it someday—maybe. (And it's been gathering dust ever since.)

- I look good in it, but I've never had anywhere to wear it. (How many of those do you need?)

- It's such an old friend, even though it's totally shredded. (Friends don't let friends look ugly.)

- Do I fit these clothes any longer? (Ah, well, hope springs eternal. Maybe next year or the year after I'll lose the weight and get down to that shape, and so on.)

If you have any clothes that fit any of those criteria, it's time to let them go (just like outmoded beliefs or behaviors). Keep only the clothes you really wear *and that are in good shape.* Toss out the ones you'll never wear, that you've worn out, that you shouldn't wear because they're out of style or look bad or you can't fit into. Those clothes reflect attitudes you have about yourself that are unrealistic, outdated, or self-deprecating, which hold you back and prevent something good from coming in, like your soulmate.

.It may take you several sessions to let go of all the clothes you really need to discard. Once you've actually managed to do it, you may discover something extraordinary—a feeling of incredible satisfaction, triumph, relief, and even fear—because you've let go of old, familiar stuff, and going out into the unknown is scary. When you get rid of things that have a hold on you, by freeing yourself of them physically, you also release a huge emotional burden as well—one you didn't even know you had.

If you've done the job right, you will end with a closet that's about a third *full*—not a third empty! The next step is to do *nothing* for at least a month. Give yourself time to get used to your new physical and emotional space, to let your mind and body adjust to the new landscape. When you finally start buying new clothes, they will begin to reflect the New You.

Lois had a wall-to-wall closet jammed with twenty years' worth of clothing. Being overweight, she also had clothes in various sizes, reflecting her fluctuating weight. She kept hoping that she would lose enough weight to wear them. I helped her recognize that even if she did get down to her ideal weight, those clothes were way out of style, so there was no point in keeping them. Besides, it was time to accept herself as she was now.

It took her a month to completely clean out her closet. By the time she finished, her closet was one-sixth full. She told me tossing out those clothes was one of the most painful experiences she had ever had because of the memories, beliefs, dreams, and fears associated with them. When it was done, she felt a huge burden had been lifted from her. It was reflected in her life in amazing ways. She shed her old relationship, her stultifying job, changed her living arrangement, and started losing weight!

It's the same thing in a soulmate relationship.

Resources

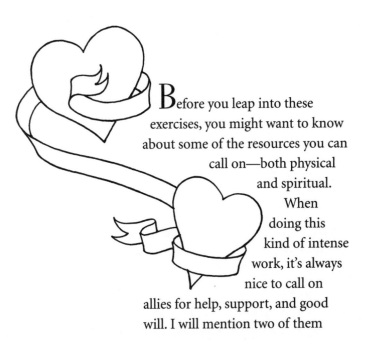

Before you leap into these exercises, you might want to know about some of the resources you can call on—both physical and spiritual. When doing this kind of intense work, it's always nice to call on allies for help, support, and good will. I will mention two of them quite often in these processes—your Higher Self and angels. What I find so important about them is their willingness to help you lovingly and without question. That makes them nonthreatening, as well.

You may not believe it now, but as you begin to work on meeting your soulmate, it is liable to bring up a lot of doubts and fears about yourself, your worthiness for a relationship, and self-judgments. Having an angel or your Higher Self beside you during the process reminds you that you are indeed lovable, and that you deserve your soulmate relationship—which makes the process safer and easier. Let me describe these resources in a little more detail.

Your Resources

Higher Self

Your Higher Self is your wise, immortal soul. It acts as the bridge between Mother/Father God and you; yet its clear messages are often hard to hear because of interference from your mind's judgments and chatter. Meditation or some other practice that stills your mind allows you to experience your Higher Self's wisdom and love.

Because it knows everything about you, it is under no illusion about you and your so-called flaws. It cannot be influenced by outsiders or your mind, or be overwhelmed by your fears and needs. You may think poorly of yourself, but your Higher Self doesn't. It wants nothing more than your greater well-being. One of its desires is for you to meet your soulmate (as long as it's in line with the highest good).

Guardian Angel

Your guardian angel is a being who has chosen to become your invisible companion. You may have one or even several guardian angels. Like your Higher Self, they have your best interests at heart, but unlike your Higher Self, they are not part of you. They may be people who loved you while they were alive, like grandparents who have come to watch over you again in discarnate form, or they may just be kind strangers.

Like your Higher Self, your guardian angel also provides wise suggestions, but its major purpose is to protect and help you in your work.

Children are very much in tune with the idea of guardian angels. In fact, those invisible friends children talk to are usually their guardian angels, providing them with loving companionship.

Angels

We hear a great deal about angels these days. Many people believe in angelic interventions even though they might not accept the idea of a Higher Self or are uncomfortable with the idea of talking to Mother/Father God. Angels are a safe intermediary. All they need is a summons from you and they will gladly lend a hand. And as minions of Mother/Father God, they bring both divine power and divine blessing into your process.

Higher Selves and angels come in many shapes, sizes, and dimensions. Some may appear as gods and goddesses; others may look like you or like simple energy forms, while some can only be sensed as invisible but tangible presences. You might not even get a sense of anything at all. But although you may not detect your Higher Self or guardian angel the first time you call on them, they are always there for you.

Exercise to Meet Your Higher Self or Your Guardian Angel

This exercise helps you connect with your Higher Self or your guardian angel. Without their help, you can do the work; but with these allies beside you, the exercises become more powerful. You can do this exercise any time, but I highly recommend that you do it before you start the soulmate exercises.

- Imagine a special place—a room furnished any way you want, a lovely forest or meadow, or a mountain or seaside. Since time and space are mutable in your imagination, you can create any landscape you want.

- Ask your Higher Self/guardian angel to meet you there. Notice what they look like. Sense their presence. You might even feel their love for you. If you do, just bathe in it.

- Let them know that you want to work on bringing your soulmate to you, and you'd like their

help. You may get a response from them, or not.
None is required.

- After awhile, open your eyes and come back,
remembering that you can call on your Higher
Self/guardian angel at any time. They are always
there.

Altar

Another resource I encourage you to have is inanimate—
an altar. It serves as a focus for your sacred objects.

Your altar is your sacred space. It may be a shelf or
table, but not a knickknack shelf. On it you display those
objects that have special, holy meaning to you. Altars are
used to evoke specific kinds of energy and invoke certain
higher beings. When you sit before it and pray or meditate,
you feel a connection with Mother/Father God, your
Higher Self, your angels, or any other transcendent beings.

Several of these exercises involve creating particular
objects. Once you've made them, you may want to keep
them on your altar as a constant reminder of what and

who you are summoning. This is particularly important when you are calling in your soulmate's essence. As you focus on one of your talismans while you are chanting, making decrees, or going through the exercises, it will enhance the power of your work.

If you prefer not to put your objects on display because you lack privacy, you think they may be disturbed, or it just feels uncomfortable, you might want to put them in a container intended specifically for your sacred objects. Don't mix them in with your everyday possessions. Soulmate work is special; it creates a special kind of energy vortex. Throwing your sacred objects in with your everyday things diminishes your work and disperses the energy you want to build up.

If you don't have an altar, you might want to consider creating one. What kind would be proper to create? It doesn't have to be elaborate. The simplest one is often a shelf or a small table where you can put your sacred objects—those items that are spiritually meaningful for you, including candles, crystals, pictures, statues, and so on. An example of one altar is on the following page.

An example of an altar.

An altar may contain any or all of the following:

- Objects from sacred sites (like Stonehenge, Mt. Shasta, Glastonbury, Egypt, Sedona)

- Picture of the Dalai Lama

- Crystals and minerals

- Sacred books (reflecting your spiritual practice)

- Statuette of Buddha or Kuan-Yin

- Angel cards

- Colored candles for burning

- Flowers

- Incenses

- Other objects that symbolize your goal

Once you place your soulmate objects on your altar, they will be imbued with the energies of this sacred space.

Supplies

Throughout the exercises, I mention using different kinds of supplies, such as love-focused incenses or other incense blends, love oil, candles of particular colors, and goddess pictures or statues. You can find these different supplies at most metaphysical or New Age stores, Indian import stores (such as Cost Plus or Pier One), herbal botanicas, and on the Internet. There is a huge and expanding market of vendors who can easily provide you with the required items, especially if the items are unavailable in your area. If you don't have a computer with a modem, use the one at your local library. They all have Internet access. Another resource is local party supply stores. You will find interesting things there, like candles, tablecloths, and mylar confetti. Refer to the list of resources at the back of this book.

Whatever resources you gather for your altar, allow your creativity and inner wisdom to make the decisions. After all, it's an expression of your self, your spirit, and your highest purpose. And this work, like anything that you put your whole spirit, mind, and body toward, will be most successful if everything you surround yourself with resonates with you and provides you with a sense of love and joy.

Preparation

Manifesting your soulmate requires a proper setting and attitude. After all, this is serious business. The first step is to provide yourself with some time, a quiet space, and few distractions. In other words, if other people are around demanding your attention, that's not a good time

37

or place for your work. In that case, you need to remove yourself to a place where you won't be disturbed.

Next, you need to prepare yourself energetically. You can't simply jump into this work. It's best to make a gentle transition from everyday reality into your sacred space. This may be achieved through practices like meditation, yoga, energy clean-out, and grounding. They help you become balanced, clear, and in a receptive mood for whatever develops.

I suggest several energy exercises that I have found helpful in preparing you and your body for processing: Grounding, Energy Clean-out, and Retrieving Your Energy.

Grounding Exercise

This is the most important exercise of all because it puts you back into your body and reminds you that you are anchored to the earth. That's actually very comforting to your physical body, which often feels like it is adrift, left to fend for itself while your mind/consciousness zips along on its own path. (That's why you may bump into things "by accident." Your consciousness was elsewhere, so your body stumbled into disaster.)

The more grounded you are, the more aware you are; which means you are more likely to sense the presence of your soulmate or your Higher Self. All your experiences will have much more meaning and power.

Here are two simple methods of grounding.

Method 1

Imagine a laser beam of light dropping from the base of your spine down through the earth and hooking into the center of the earth. Let it expand in width until it is a column wider than your whole body. Then let that beam of light extend upward until it connects with the sun.

Method 2

Imagine Mother Earth's hands coming up from the earth and surrounding you, holding you gently in her hands (see illustration, next page).

This grounding method is particularly good when you are feeling frazzled, upset, or spacy, and you're having a

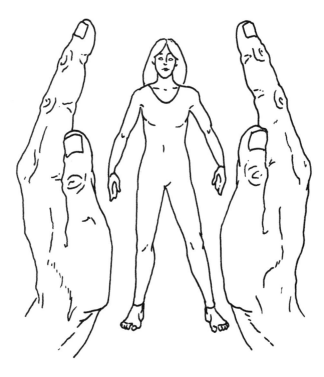

Grounding Method 2: Letting Mother Earth's
hands gently ground you.

difficult time thinking, never mind grounding! Letting Mother Earth ground you is very comforting and easy. She does the work.

Energy Clean-out Exercise

Cleaning out your personal space is essential for this work. Most of us walk around collecting other people's energies, and we don't even know it. We get that way by interacting with people, talking, even walking around—in other words, daily living. It's best for only you to be involved with your soulmate, not you and all the people who have left their energy in your aura (the eighteen inches of energy around your body). Simply cleaning out your aura every day will make an enormous difference.

The clean-out also helps you define your personal boundary. It declares, "This is my space. I belong here, and everybody else belongs out there." It does not isolate you from others since you can choose to let special friends inside.

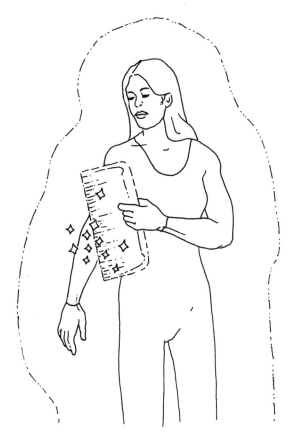

Cleaning out the aura.

- To clean all the foreign energies from your space (i.e., anyone who isn't you), imagine holding a large golden comb with eighteen-inch teeth, which you will use to brush out your aura. Physically move your hands up and down your body from head to foot, like you're combing out floor-length hair.

- As you comb through your aura, let the debris that is being removed fall onto the earth, where it can be recycled as neutral energy.

- Let a large golden ball of sunlight form above your head. As it slides down into your body and spreads its healing light out to the edge of your aura, it forms a kind of golden force field around you. You have now cleaned and defined your space.

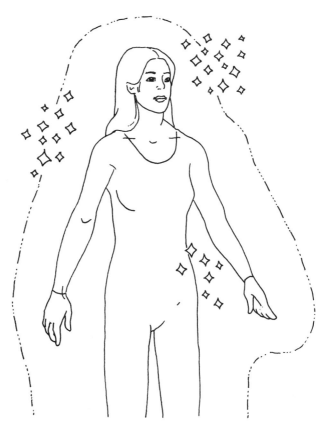

Other people's energy within an aura.

Retrieving Your Energy Exercise

Since foreign energy gets stuck in your aura, it's only logical to assume that you leave your energy in other places, as well. This next technique calls your missing energy back to you.

- Close your eyes and imagine you have an energy whistle, like an ultra-high-pitched dog whistle. Blow it to call your energy home.

- After a few moments, pieces of energy will start flowing back to you; they may appear or feel like snowflakes, blobs or sparkles.

- Take about five minutes to allow your energy to come back. You might suddenly get memories from years ago. That means your energy had been left in those experiences.

It's very important to do all of these exercises every day for maximum benefit. In any case, I strongly suggest you to do them all before doing any of the exercises.

The Snapshot

How will you know that these processes have made a difference in your life? You won't—unless you have a Before and After picture. It's like seeing those dieting pictures with the dramatic weight change. Like them, you will have gone through a deep transformation by the time you've completed the book, but you may not notice. While you're in the middle of your work, it's often hard to track the inner change. It only becomes obvious in the kind of answers you give to certain questions, which reflect your shift in attitudes, beliefs, and feelings.

That's why, before you start the exercises, I suggest that you create a kind of snapshot of yourself. It will help you actually chart your personal growth.

Use this form to fill in the specific personal information requested. I don't want you to make an inventory of your bad traits. The point of this list is to give you a sense of what you're like *right* now in all kinds of ways—how you feel about yourself, what you are like, what your dreams are, your good points, your ideals, and your personal obstacles.

Since this information is for you alone, the only one who needs to see it is you. That means it's best to be as honest as you can. If you aren't, you'll be the one who's shortchanging yourself.

Copy this form on a piece of paper, and fill it out. Don't lose it.

The Snapshot Form

Likes, in general (about anything)	Dislikes, in general (about anything)
Personal qualities you like	Personal qualities you dislike
Characteristics (what makes you different from everyone else in the world)	What the ideal you would look and be like
Fears (personal and global)	Ideal mate
Hopes and dreams (personal and for others)	Ideal world (business and home)
Spiritual beliefs	What is important to you

Once you've completed your inventory, put it away until you've finished the book. In the conclusion you'll get to do another list, and you can compare those answers with this one.

Before You Start

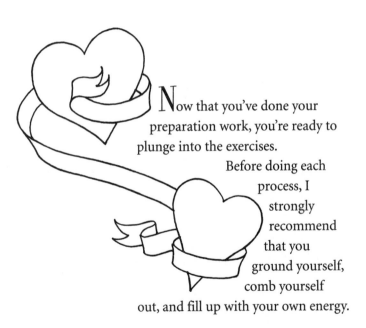

Now that you've done your preparation work, you're ready to plunge into the exercises.

Before doing each process, I strongly recommend that you ground yourself, comb yourself out, and fill up with your own energy.

The more of your own life-force energy you have, the stronger impact the exercise will have for you and for your soulmate.

For each exercise I give a suggested length for the process—no more than an hour. If you continue the process any longer than that, the focus of your work dissipates, and so does your energy. That's not what you want.

You may find yourself wanting to adapt some of the exercises to fit your own purposes or needs. What I have given you is a guideline, using steps that I know work. But this is your work, and you know yourself. You may discover or conceive a variation that you prefer. Feel free to make those adaptations. After all, it's your life and your soulmate.

Have fun with the exercises. Grow and enjoy.

Good luck.

How to Do the Exercises

You might want a guide to proceed through the processes. Here is a suggested course based on your level of interest and concern. I have set up four categories, from Very Tentative to Really Committed, with the exercises that I suggest you try for each category.

Very Tentative
If you're completely new at this kind of work, and are not sure what you might be getting into, do the following exercises:

2, 3, 11, 12, 15, 16, 18, 19

Tentative
If you're exploring the possibility of having a soulmate relationship, and aren't sure you're ready, do the following exercises:

1, 3, 6, 9, 11, 12, 13, 15, 16, 18, 19

Committed
If you're ready, but still want to go slowly, do the following exercises:

1, 2, 4, 5, 7, 8, 9, 10, 11, 12, 13, 14, 15, 16, 17, 18, 19

Really Committed
It's time! Do any and all of them.

Willingness Exercise

As a test of your willingness to bring your soulmate into your life, you might want to do the following exercise.

- Imagine a television screen; on it are two blobs of light, a red one (you) and a blue one (your soulmate).

- Let the two blobs drift toward each other. How do they approach each other? Is it fast or slow? Do they merge or just touch each other, or is there some kind of space between them? Notice what happens.

- If they merge, you're ready for a relationship. If they're touching, you're more tentative. If they don't want to get close, you're not even sure you want to get involved with them. Hopefully, that will change as you do your work.

The Exercises

Exercise 1

Calling in Your Soulmate's Essence

The soulmate essence exercise is the core exercise in this book. From it stem almost all the other exercises. The main purpose of this exercise is to let you touch your soulmate's energy— perhaps for the first time ever. That puts you both on notice that you DO have a soulmate, and you are working to create a link with them. Each time you make that connection, you forge a bond between you two. You may see or sense them, whatever is most comfortable to you.

At this point, I'm sure some of you are thinking, "What if I don't sense/see/feel anything?" That's entirely possible. Even though their essence is actually touching you, it's your mind that is blocking you from percieving them. I've mentioned that the idea of meeting your soulmate may be very scary because it will entail changes in your life. One way to protect yourself is not to sense anything when you call in your soulmate.

Regardless of what you see or sense, just continue to summon your soulmate essence anyway and pretend your soulmate is there. It doesn't matter that you notice nothing! It's the act of calling it in that's critical because it shows intent—your intent—to make this connection.

Not only that—at the same time, you are beginning the process of personal change in preparation for the actual physical manifestation.

It's entirely possible that you may not see or sense your soulmate for a few sessions. That's quite common. Sooner or later, you will "suddenly" sense or see your soulmate. By the time that happens, you'll have confronted a lot of your own inner fears. And they will come up!

Especially the first time, as you wait to meet your soulmate, you're likely to hear inner voices objecting, complaining, arguing. These are parts of you that have some fear of this process or investment in the status quo. In fact, each one has *its* own agenda, which may or may not have any relevance to *your* best interests. One of them is having you remain as you are now.

When you meet your soulmate in body, a lot of things are going to be different. These inner parts are afraid they won't know what to do when you change, which is all for the good.

The best way to handle those inner voices is to acknowledge them. Simply thank each of them for sharing their comments with you. If you think this won't work, you'll be surprised. It's like a toddler pulling at your leg for attention; once you acknowledge them, they go away. Until you do, however, they'll get more and more insistent.

That's one of the reasons to bring your Higher Self or an angel into this meeting. They can bring your soulmate to you, lend a hand in coping with these inner parts, and generally make you feel safer. Meeting your soulmate may be quite unsettling (as the voices in your head fear), so having your support team around you will be very comforting. It's like they're disinterested but loving facilitators between you and your soulmate. Having your Higher Self or an angel at the meetings, to ease you into the process, is always safer and more comforting.

Duration: 30 minutes.

- Find a quiet place away from distractions—at home alone; in a natural setting; or somewhere quiet, like a library. Put on soft meditative music, if possible. Take a few deep releasing breaths.

- Close your eyes.

- Do the Grounding, Energy Clean-out, and Retrieving Your Energy exercises (see page 38).

- Imagine yourself in a special place that makes you feel good; it may be a special room or somewhere in nature (lake, forest, ocean, mountain, meadow). Wherever you are, you feel at ease. Take a few moments to relax in that special environment. Breathe in the scents of the flowers and plants or the ocean's salty tang; listen to the sounds of the animals, the chirping birds, the rustling of the tree leaves, the lapping of the water. Let your senses get in tune with that world. Take a few more deep rhythmic breaths.

- Call in your Higher Self/angel. In a moment you'll notice their presence, whether you see, feel, or sense them. Let them touch your shoulder or heart or hand to give you the reassurance of their presence. (If you don't sense them the first time, you will sooner or later.)

- Ask them to bring your soulmate's essence into your space. You may become aware of something or someone coming toward you. Don't forget to keep breathing! It's not an ogre!

- Meanwhile, you may notice your inner voices objecting, complaining, arguing. Just thank them for sharing their comments with you. And breathe!

- Return your focus to your soulmate. Invite their essence to approach your body. If you feel so inclined, imagine them embracing or even enfolding you. If any of this feels a little uncomfortable or overwhelming, just accept as much of their essence as you are willing to let in. It's wise to make this connection slowly. You have plenty of time to get more intimate.*

---

* If you want to use a tape of this exercise, you can order my guided meditation "Meeting Your Soulmate's Essence" (see page 252).

Exercise 2

Making a List

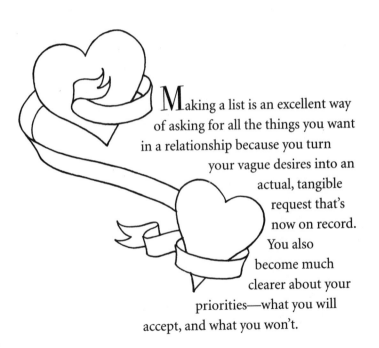

Making a list is an excellent way of asking for all the things you want in a relationship because you turn your vague desires into an actual, tangible request that's now on record. You also become much clearer about your priorities—what you will accept, and what you won't.

I wrote earlier that it is important to shed the beliefs, fears, patterns, and traumas that stand in the way of your soulmate relationship, for they prevent you from attracting that one special love relationship.

One way they affect you is in your preconceptions of a desired partner. It's the difference between your "ideal mate" and your "right mate." Your right mate is usually not your ideal. But before you get to the *right*, you have to deal with the *ideal*; without confronting and releasing the ideal, you are likely to screen out your soulmate.

Ideals come from somewhere; they don't just happen. They're an amalgam of beliefs, needs, and patterns from your childhood and youth that you have absorbed. From them you mold your image of your ideal mate. Thereafter, you compare each person you meet to this ideal. The problem is that your ideal has, generally, qualities you believe you lack (she'll be calm while I bounce off walls; he'll be generous while I pinch pennies).

That ideal is as a reaction to something from your past, so you are likely to activate a program that attracts a person who's not your ideal, and is often its opposite. How do I know that? More than one person has told me, "I attract exactly the opposite of my ideal."

Take a look at the important relationships in your life. How many of them match your ideal, and how many are opposite? It's like saying, "My father was like that, so I will look for the opposite."

Let's take shyness as an example. If you're shy, you're probably going to want your mate to act as a buffer against the world, easing your entry into conversations. What you often find, however, is someone who not only is unwilling to support you, but even embarrasses or ridicules you in public.

Your soulmate, on the other hand, is something else altogether, a unique individual who is neither your ideal nor your nightmare. Yet you won't be able to find that out until you climb off the seesaw of ideal/reality. That's why doing this list is so important. You need to uncover the old patterns and release them.

The list chips away at this ideal/reality dynamic. Not only does it make you aware of what you're unconsciously looking for, it also frees your energy from being bound up in that ideal. (If you are always attracting people who are wrong for you, there is no room for the right one to come into your life.) That, in turn, opens you up to a new kind of relationship with someone who is right for you. And no one is more right than your soulmate.

What do you need to do?

You need to list all the qualities that make up your ideal mate and compare them to the kind of person you are attracting. In this exercise, you get to track your ideals and reality, and recalibrate them both so that you are attracting neither kind.

Supplies: 3 sheets of paper; a pen.

Duration: 1 hour.

- Turn a piece of paper sideways (landscape), and divide it into three columns.

- In column one, list everything you want in an ideal mate. Hopefully, you will have a long list. It may take more than a few minutes to dredge it up, but I guarantee you have certain criteria.
  Example: "My ideal is intelligent."

Ideal	Opposite	Actual

- In column two, write down the opposite of that ideal:

    "Stupid/dumb."

    Continue finding the opposite of each positive quality, until you have done them all.

- In column three, you get to decide how your last partner fits column one or two. Which one of those qualities did they manifest—intelligence or stupidity? Maybe they're smart in business and stupid in relationships (focus on the relationship part). The smartest people often

have no common sense. That's a kind of
stupidity. Or they're intelligent but unaware.
Is that what you are attracting?

- Please be as honest as possible about the
qualities in your last partner. After all, this
exercise is in your own best interests.

- Once you've finished with column three,
circle everything that matches the ideals
in column one.

- Underline or highlight all the items of column
three that match column two.

- Now study the whole picture. This is a map of
your internal relationships—what you attract,
and what your ideal is. How does it look? How
do you feel seeing it? What are you aware of?

- Take another piece of paper. Write down a
release affirmation that converts each negative
into a positive: "I release 'stupid/dumb' from my

life." Go down the whole list and convert all the negatives into positive affirmations.

- Pick five or six affirmations and repeat each of them, individually, ten to twenty times. (Don't do all of them at the same time. It gets overwhelming.)

- When you've finished your chosen affirmations, imagine sunlight pouring down on you and filling up your body with golden light. Since gold is the highest healing color, it helps rebalance your inner cellular structure.

- Now call in your soulmate essence (exercise 1). Tune into what kind of qualities your soulmate has. Write your impressions down on a new piece of paper. This is very important because as you clean out the patterns of your ideal and its opposite, you become more attuned to what your soulmate's energy really is.

An Ideal Journey

The next step is to make an inner journey to remove those ideals from within you. By doing this inner journey, you make your affirmations stronger and you accelerate the speed of the release.

- Close your eyes. Imagine you're on an escalator going down to your heart.

- Step off and go into a small room where you store your list of ideals. It may be in a file folder, a drawer, a book, et cetera. Pull it out.

- Tear up the list into little pieces and burn them. Watch as the flames curl the paper so that they turn black and blow away. Say goodbye to those outdated ideals.

Exercise 3

Inviting Your Soulmate Into Your Life

Considering your desire to bring your soulmate into your life, it's important at this moment to stop and answer a pivotal question: Do you really want them there? "What? Of course I do!" you answer. It's an automatic response, and it may even be true . . . to some extent.

71

But—and it's a big But—that may not necessarily be your unconscious reality. Even though your mind may say, "I'll gladly let in my soulmate," somehow it never occurs. No matter how much your mind might crave the psychic touch of your soulmate, they have not come to you.

Here are two possible reasons for that situation:

- You're putting up obstacles because you're not emotionally ready to let your soulmate into your life. You still have some healing to do.

- Even if your heart really is ready for your soulmate, your lifestyle may not allow it. You simply don't have the time or energy to deal with *any* relationship, never mind such a significant one as your soulmate.

In this day and age, our lifestyles determine much of our ability to have a good loving partner. We have only so much energy available; how can we parcel it out among work, activities, family, and lover without reaching burnout? A number of people I know don't even bother to get into relationships because they simply haven't got the time. Their work or their children are all-consuming. Even though they may bemoan their inability to have a relationship—never mind find their soulmate—they won't change their situation because that is their higher priority right now.

That's what this exercise addresses: How willing (or able) are you to let your soulmate share your life? If you say you're trying to manifest a relationship, and yet you're pushing it away unconsciously, it's important to learn why—does it frighten you, or do you just not have time?

To find out the answer, you get to take your soulmate on a tour of your life, your family, your job, and your activities, and notice how well your soulmate fits with you. That will let you see what's motivating you, what you're ready for, and what's in the way.

It also brings hidden agendas out in the open so you can examine your fears, needs, and expectations. If you discover that you don't want to welcome your soulmate at this time, don't take it as a bad sign. On the contrary! Your unconscious motivations are now out in the open, and they can be dealt with on a conscious level—not attacked, but examined.

You may need to take time to adjust to the idea of having your soulmate in your life. It's better to go slow and accustom yourself to future changes than actually meet your soulmate and have the relationship fail. In that case, just doing the soulmate essence exercise (1) or the chanting (5) or decree work (6) may be enough for the time being.

In this exercise, you'll be calling on your soulmate. Though you don't know what your soulmate looks like, it doesn't matter. You can simply imagine a special lover; the reactions will still be the same on your part. In point of fact, when you meet your soulmate, you may have none of these reactions, but that's not what you're looking for. This exercise examines your expectations and fears, what goes on inside you, not the reality of a relationship.

Duration: 30 minutes.

- Find yourself a comfortable chair or couch.
  Don't lie down on the bed or floor; you're
  apt to fall asleep.

- Put on soft music. Do the Grounding, Energy Clean-out, and Retrieving Your Energy exercises (page 38).

- Close your eyes. Imagine that there is a door in front of you. As you pass through the door, you find yourself at your job. As you perform your daily routine, imagine that your soulmate is on the phone calling you. What's it like to talk with them for those few minutes, sharing intimacies ("I love you"), or just making a connection ("Hi, how are you?")? Notice if you feel grateful or harried, happy or pushed. They propose getting together for dinner. What's your reaction—are you glad? Happy? Do you wish they'd picked another night because you've got all this work? Or you're just too tired? Or, not again!

- Now the work day is over. You come out of your office building, and you see them waiting for you. What's your reaction—disappointment that they're there? Happiness? Tiredness? Anxiety? Eagerness?

- You spend the dinner talking and hanging out, and then they come home with you for a while. What's it like having them in your house? How do you feel with them beside you? Comfortable? Crowded? Harried? When they kiss you, do you lean into the kiss wholeheartedly, or is your mind somewhere else, like on the project you need to do for work, or the 1,001 things that haven't gotten done because you're spending time with them? (Yes, I'm focusing on the negative aspects because I want you to be honest with yourself. It's all right not to be wildly happy—and it's great when you are.) If none of these negative emotions come up, you're certainly more open to a relationship.

- They propose spending the weekend together. What's your immediate reaction? Yes! Oh, no! I suppose (gee, such enthusiasm).

- If you have children, imagine letting your soul-mate meet them. What's your reaction now? Are

you dreading the meeting? Or is it joyful, fun?
Do your children want someone new in their
life? If you don't have kids, substitute close
friends or pets. (Pay attention to your pet's
reaction. They're often wiser than we are.)

- Finally, imagine your soulmate sitting beside
  you, saying, "I want us to get married." What's
  your response to that? Perhaps the first reaction
  will be elation. But after that initial spurt of joy,
  what else do you feel? Do you have mixed
  emotions? Dread? Contentment? Happiness?
  Rightness?

- Now they've gone home, and you are sitting in
  this very chair you're doing this exercise in.
  Imagine that you can see your soulmate's
  essence; it's a bright green. It's floating around
  your home, as if saying, "I'm here with you at all
  times." How does that make you feel, knowing
  that they are always near you? Comforted?
  Hemmed in? Overwhelmed? Relaxed?

- Your reaction to all these questions indicates how ready you are to let them into your life. Remember, there is no right or wrong answer. It's just your feelings, which you need to honor. And if you find out you're not ready for that relationship yet, consider yourself lucky. You have the opportunity now to deal with the fears and worries that are keeping that partner away.

Exercise 4

Attraction Template

Let's imagine that inside of us are patterns that we have created from beliefs, fears, needs, and desires. We have many patterns that, once they have been formed, guarantee that we'll act and react in a certain way. Patterns include our personal style— our choices for food, entertainment, relationships, friendships, outlook, beliefs. Even if you were to change your identity, it would be far more difficult to change your patterns. Your identity is skin deep, but your patterns are embedded inside you.

Because you want to work on attracting your soulmate, we're going to be examining a particular pattern, the one having to do with relationships and the kind of person you're looking for. I call it the attraction template. Once it is constructed, it forces you to respond in certain predictable ways. (It's like having to use a door to go out of your house. The walls restrict your movement. You can't walk through them!)

The attraction template has been formulated to allow you to have relationships with a certain kind of person— and to ignore all the others that don't fit its criteria. It is an amalgamation of patterns from childhood needs— particularly around love, safety, attention, self-worth, shame, self-importance, independence. If you were always looking for love as a child because you never felt you got enough, you're going to be looking for a lover who will provide you with an unlimited bounty of love. But unfortunately, since you only have this one pattern of trying to get love from someone who doesn't give you enough, that's the kind of person you'll find!

That's what those holes are—the doors of your house, which let in only certain kinds of people. In my workshops I describe the attraction template as a board with six square holes. In actuality, for most people, their templates are as personal as they are, with their own unique image. What is important about the attraction template is the shape of those holes. You can only have a successful relationship with a person who fits into your square holes. They are kinds of compatibility: Attitudes about marriage, child rearing, parenting, communication, intimacy, empowerment, manipulation, love and sex, money (this is a big one)—in other words, everything that makes up the normal range of interpersonal issues, all of which are influenced or derived from early experiences or learning. (Obviously, since there are a lot more than six items that make up a relationship, there are lots more holes. But this is, of course, just an example.)

That means only square pegs can go into square holes, not any other shape. Should they have only five square

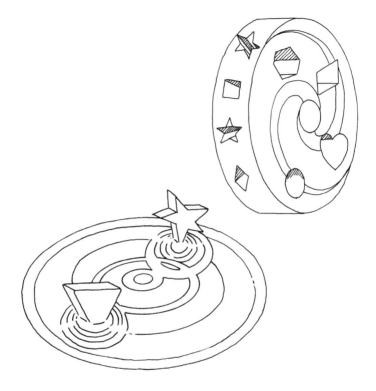

Examples of attraction templates expanded
to include new possibilities.

pegs, you probably will do just fine together, except for a few points of incompatibility.

Suppose you meet someone who has lots of other shapes, like circles, triangles, rectangles, crescents, crosses, as well as a few square pegs? You two aren't really compatible. They might become a short-term relationship, but there's not enough to sustain a relationship. If there are no matches at all, you won't get together. (Think of an intellectual and an outdoors type; they don't mesh well, and their values are often quite different.)

What if you happen to meet the soulmate you've been praying for so diligently? Even if you are literally standing next to each other, and make eye contact or exchange a few words, the spark won't be there. The attraction templates are out of alignment with each other.

If by some miracle you do make contact, you won't be able to maintain a relationship with them. It's like wearing out-of-focus glasses. They prevent you from seeing objects clearly—in this case, your soulmate. Remember exercise 2, where you made the list of the expectations you had about your ideal lover? Those expectations, needs, and patterns are hardwired into your chakras.

The word "chakra" comes from the Sanskrit word for "wheel." The chakras are energy centers in our body, each one focusing on a particular kind of energy. The ability we have to function in a holistic way is directly connected to how clogged or unclogged our chakras are. I see chakras according to the classic Indian model:

First chakra: at the base of your spine; survival issues (money, shelter, job, health)

Second chakra: three inches below your navel; sex and emotions

Third chakra: solar plexus (just below your diaphragm); power and control

Fourth chakra: heart; love

Fifth chakra: throat, ears, mouth; communication

Sixth chakra: center of your head, third eye; clear seeing

Seventh chakra: top of head; wisdom

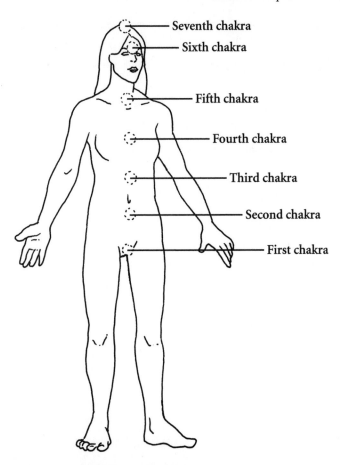

The seven chakras.

It doesn't matter what you think you want; you can't change the program—unless you want to. To make yourself attractive or irresistible to your soulmate, you need to change the templates in each of the chakras to accept that particular energy. That means going into each chakra, finding the attraction template, and cleaning it off or replacing it. Whatever you choose to do to the template, you are making a decision to move from lack, fear, or constriction to openness and empowerment on all levels.

Elias found that his template was very small (two holes). After he cleaned it off, his Higher Self told him to open it, and it doubled in size, then doubled again and again, until it was huge, with holes of all shapes and sizes.

Bert's new attraction template looked like a spinning wheel with hundreds of new openings.

Jane's attraction template was a pool of silver that allowed her to accept all kinds of new energies.

When you create a brand new template, or even upgrade the old one, you are, in effect, creating something brand new inside yourself, something that reflects a different *you* of a much higher order. That means the old energies and patterns inside you will have difficulty functioning because they are at the old vibration level. It's like loading new powerful software that overloads the system so you have to upgrade everything else.

The result is that your body may become overwhelmed; its way of handling the load is often to get sick (flu, fever, cold, sore throat—to use the computer metaphor, it's downtime). During this period of illness, your body gets the opportunity to discard the programs or patterns that no longer have any validity in your life. That's why, once you recover from a cold or flu, you often feel better spiritually, if not physically, at least at first.

When you find your attraction template, you may want to get rid of it . . . or you may not. If you choose to retain your old template, that's because you want to make changes at a more deliberate pace, and you're not ready to get rid of old familiar friends. Honor that decision. Throwing away your old attraction template and replacing it with a new one is definitely an act of finality.

Once you've done the process of release, you also get to do the process of invitation—in this case, your soulmate's essence. That means once you have altered the old rigid patterns, you can invite your soulmate into that chakra and infuse the template with its energies. Then your template will be keyed to allow that most important and attractive pattern into your life.

When you do this process, work on one chakra at a time. That gives your body some time to adjust to the new energies before tackling the attraction template in another chakra. Remember, you are removing old patterns (just like you cleaned out your closet), and taking on new ones. You need time to adjust to the new vibration.

You may notice that the templates in each chakra appear different—or they may be identical from chakra to chakra. Whatever comes up is just exactly what's right for you.

Duration: 30 minutes.

- Put on some meditative music. Get comfortable.

- Do the Grounding, Energy Clean-out, and Retrieving Your Energy exercises (page 38).

- Call in your Higher Self or angel.

- Call on your soulmate's essence.

- Imagine yourself stepping onto an escalator from the center of your head; let it carry you down to your chosen chakra. Whatever you see there is symbolic—it's not the actual physical organ.

- Find the attraction template on the chakra wall or wherever it's located.

- Ask your Higher Self to bring in a vat of gold liquid.

- Fill a bucket with that gold liquid and dump it over the attraction template. The gold liquid acts as a transformative lubricant that loosens the template from the wall.

- Pry the template off the wall, with your Higher Self's help, if necessary.

- Drop it into the vat. If there are other pieces of hardware, like screws or plates that keep your template bolted to the wall, throw them into the vat as well; they belong to the old way of thinking and need to be discarded.

- Take the template out of the vat. Observe its condition. If your attraction template looks pretty
  good after its bath, and you don't want to get rid
  of it, you can retain it—for now. Just check to
  make sure that it has more holes (options).

- If it is thin, broken, torn, cracked, or holey,
  dump it back into the vat. It's no good. You need
  a new attraction template.

- Ask your Higher Self to provide a new template,
  one that reflects you and your energy now.

- Hang the new or refurbished template on
  the wall.

- Let your soulmate put their essence into your
  template so it can recognize their pattern. You
  might imagine them laying their hands on the
  template to infuse it with their energy.

- Do this technique in each chakra—but not all at
  the same time. Allow yourself a separate session
  for each one.*

* You can also use the guided meditation "Who You Attract"
  (see page 252).

Exercise 5

Chanting

When you think of chanting, what comes to mind? Monks and Gregorian chants? Indian gurus? Native Americans? All of them chant. Chanting has a religious overtone—you chant in some holy setting, like a temple or ashram or church. No matter what kinds of chanting they do, the purpose is the same: To create some kind of change in your body and mind.

Chanting is a combination of word and song, specifically a series of words (mantras) sung over and over again to evoke in you a kind of uplifting vibration that will put you in harmony with the transcendent energies that are attracted by your singing.

Chanting performs three major functions. First, it quiets your mind with its rather complex repetitive phrases. You're not chanting a one-word mantra, but two to three sentences at least. Unlike a spoken affirmation, a chant is intoned or shouted out in song. In fact, the more you sing it out, the more you put your heart in the song, the stronger the body experience.

Second, it focuses your mind on a particular being, event, process, goal, or ideal. This is very important because in so much of our life we are scattered, frustrated, fragmented. That's why chanting can be so powerful; we're drawn into a musical rhythm, the sounds of the words (which we may not understand since they are often in a foreign language), and the power of the energy created by the chanting for a period of time, at least twenty to thirty minutes. The music itself is usually a droning, rhythmic, or simple pattern of notes.

Third, a chant puts you in a different mind space. It dislodges you from preconceived beliefs and patterns, and it disengages your inner voices (like your inner Judge) so you are open to consider alternatives that your mind might not normally allow.

Since chanting is a kind of self-hypnosis, it leaves you open to suggestion, so whatever you are chanting about creates a magnetic field of attraction and possibility around you.

I chant whenever I'm doing something that is mindless or repetitive. Since I'm going to be spacing out, or thinking about something else other than what I'm doing, I might as well be doing something that will benefit me rather than just wasting mental and spiritual time. One of the best times for me is when I'm walking. It puts me into a frame of mind of openness, receptivity, and spiritual alignment. Also, it helps me organize my thoughts, which tend to ramble all over the place.

I am going to suggest two chants that you might use. But if you have your own words or sentiments you wish to express, please feel free to use them instead. This is not great poetry, but that's not the purpose. It expresses what you want to manifest.

Chant Examples

1: My arms are open; my soulmate is near.
   Come into my arms; and be with me here.

2: I am ready for my soulmate; let my lover come to me.
   I am ready for my soulmate; let my lover embrace me.
   I am open to my soulmate; I invite him/her in my life. (I know it's not grammatical, but it fits.)
   I am open for my soulmate; let my lover come to me.

Don't just mouth the words. Adapt the chant to some kind of singsong music so that you're singing the words.

You're apt to find, as you say the words in a kind of singsong, that a melody will present itself. The words create their song.

Nor should you just rattle off the words, at least at first. Give yourself time to speak the words mindfully. That again adds focus to your work. Then, as you get more familiar with the chant, sing it louder and faster. That raises your energy and focus as well.

Sing more than one chant, just like you say more than one affirmation, and keep rotating them. Create a repertoire of several chants.

One woman, Jean, sang the second chant ("I am ready for my soulmate") for five minutes every few hours. She chose this chant because she knew she wasn't ready. Yet, as she continued her daily chanting, she felt a strange sense of peace with herself, and her anxiety and fears began to diminish. Eventually, she really did feel ready for her soulmate.

If you develop chants you'd like to share with others, e-mail me at arians@rocketmail.com, so I can post them on my webpage.

Exercise 6

Decrees and Affirmations

Affirmations are statements that, as you say them, are supposed to activate positive feelings within you and create the desired positive results. However, before they do that, they do something else: They activate your negative programming, so you're in the middle of what you don't want.

Even though the affirmation may seem to be giving you the exact opposite of what you're asking for, in fact, it's doing exactly the right thing by stirring up the muck. You get an opportunity to bring into sharper focus the beliefs and fears that are holding you back, so you can clean them out of yourself. Once they go away, the affirmations start working.

Usually, we say many repetitions of an affirmation at one time. This keeps the focus on a particular desire that you want to manifest, or a block that you are seeking to release or to resolve. That stirs up the negativity (at first) and then later stimulates you to align with what the affirmation proposes.

Decrees are affirmations with an attitude: A lot of oomph is necessary. I WILL BE/HAVE/DO THAT! (And nothing can stop me!) That's because a decree is more energetically focused and intense than an affirmation. It is a function of your intent and will. You are declaring forcefully that such and such will occur.

Since the words are not sung, it is not a chant. Yet the idea is similar. By strongly declaring what you want, you create a kind of psychic ultrasound wave inside of you that is as effective in breaking up blocks as regular ultrasound is in breaking up kidney stones and cataracts.

As you repeat your decrees, they hammer against the parts of you that are not in alignment with the sentiment. At first, you likely will have a reaction against your affirmation. Then, as you persist with your decrees, the old patterns become fragmented and space opens up for new ways of thinking and feeling.

At the same time, your affirmation is sending energy outward to your soulmate as well.

What would you like to decree? I have provided a few suggestions, but again, adapt them to your own needs and situation.

As always, it's important to call in your soulmate's essence before you begin. Then, as you are decreeing, feel your soulmate receiving the benefit of your affirmations, as if they are bouncing around in their aura. In response, imagine that they are sending your their own affirmation of love as well to reinforce your own work.

Decree Examples

1: I decree that my soulmate is coming to me, that I release anything that stands in their way, and that I am ready for the relationship. I decree that it is a wonderful experience for both of us.

2: I decree that my soulmate is here; that we are together, happy, loving, and strongly committed.

3: I decree that my soulmate and I have found each other, that I have let go of all my blocks and fears, and so has he/she, and our relationship is long-lasting, loving, and caring.

4: I decree that all my fears and obstacles are gone, freeing me for a loving relationship with my soulmate.

5: I call on my Higher Self (or angels, or whatever being you would like to substitute) to do whatever is necessary to prepare me for my soulmate.

Make up your own decrees that fit the particular situation as you go along.

Whenever you say your decrees, throw yourself into the process. Proclaim them to the world. Let the walls reverberate with the joy and love you feel as you say them. The more you decree, and the more you feel the words, the more engaged your whole being becomes. Your energy rises. You really feel those words. I like to say twenty-five iterations of the same affirmation at a time. That gets my energy moving.

Reversal

There are some people for whom decrees and affirmations don't work. Their internal wiring is reversed. What that means is that their early patterns have set up a negative field so that everything you say that's positive becomes a negative; "You're lovely" becomes "You're ugly." "My soulmate is here" becomes "My soulmate will never come." This internal wiring has become so embedded that it takes more than affirmations or decrees to break it loose.

To counteract this reversal, rub the edge of your palm about one inch below the little finger joint. That will help short-circuit the negative field so that you can receive the benefit of your decree.

Exercise 7

Dreaming Your Soulmate Into Reality

In exercise 1, we talked about calling your soulmate's essence to you to create a connection with them. Now you will discover another powerful tool for making that connection: Using your imagination to dream their existence. It requires you to get into a place of receptivity to your lover, your soulmate. You want your soulmate to connect with you on all levels—emotional, spiritual, mental, etheric, and physical—so you can be in alignment with each other. This inner imagery engages all of your senses so you create a visceral, emotional, and visual connection to your soulmate.

The first time you do this exercise, you may not feel very much at all, and your visualization may be vague, at best. Don't despair. As you continue doing this exercise, over time your feeling sense will deepen, as will your visualization, so that both become much stronger and clearer.

If you receive no visual image or feeling sense, let your imagination supply it. Don't force it. It doesn't matter whether that picture is accurate or not. What's important is that you are creating a vortex of energy that magnetizes your soulmate to you. As you continue doing this exercise over the weeks, you will find your picture sharpening and changing as you tune into what they really are like.

Not only that, you will find yourself becoming more focused and attuned to this other entity. You may even notice strange sensations or ideas coming into your mind about them. These are the result of the strengthening connection between you. Not only are you sensing them, but they are sensing you as well. It will all be clear in time— when you two actually meet. By then, you will know each other so well, you can't *help* but click!

This exercise may be done standing with your eyes closed, or you may do it in front of a full-length mirror. If you use the mirror, imagine as you look at yourself that someone, that special lover, is joining you in the mirror. As you follow the steps of the exercise, you can actually see them coming along with you.

It takes a powerful focus to use the mirror, but somehow, it does make the experience even more intense. Perhaps it's because as you see your body doing the steps of the process, it engages your mind and emotions while you call your soulmate into existence in the mirror. Eventually, of course, they will step out into this reality.

Do the exercise standing up. That's how I personally like it. It's a very satisfying experience.

Supplies: Sage incense; patchouli or jasmine incense; love oil.

Duration: 15–30 minutes.

- Put on your soft music.

- Do the Grounding, Energy Clean-out, and Retrieving Your Energy exercises (page 38).

- Burn some sage incense to break down and release any old energies around and inside you. You want your own energy in the beginning.

- This time you're going to stand in bare feet while doing this process.

- Light the patchouli or jasmine incense.

- Drop a couple love oil drops onto the incense so that the love vibration permeates the room.

- Call in your soulmate's essence.

- You may want to close your eyes; it's easier to visualize that way. Imagine your soulmate coming toward you until they are standing before (not to the side or behind) you. It's as though you are meeting each other. If you're doing this in the mirror, imagine them approaching you.

- Take the love oil and anoint yourself. Put it on each of the chakras (see figure, page 85). Start from your seventh (crown) chakra. As you do, imagine lines of energy are being formed between you and your soulmate from each of these chakras, with the energies sizzling back and forth across these lines. Say the following:

  "I am connecting with my soulmate from my seventh chakra, spirit to spirit."

  "I am connecting with my soulmate, in my sixth chakra, mind to mind."

  "I'm connecting with my soulmate, in my fifth chakra, telepathically."

"I'm connecting with my soulmate, in my fourth chakra, heart to heart."

"I'm connecting with my soulmate, in my third chakra, in my power."

"I'm connecting with my soulmate, in my second chakra, sexually."

"I'm connecting with my soulmate, in my first chakra, with my body and in all my basic needs."

- Anoint your feet. Say, "I'm solidly on the earth, grounded and ready for my love."

- Anoint your palms. Say, "I'm connecting with my soulmate through my hands."

- Run your hands around your aura. Say, "My aura is filled with their energy."

- Focus on your soulmate. Sense how tall they are; what shape they have; what their hair is like and how it feels when you touch it. Run your hands along their body; notice what it's like touching them. Imagine their hands; reach out and clasp them. What kind of grip do they have?

- Let the energy course through your body. Notice where you feel most open, and where your energy feels the most blocked. That indicates where you are ready to welcome your soulmate, and where you are not, as yet. Keep breathing.

- When you feel complete, fold your hands across and over your shoulders to end the energy exchange. Thank your soulmate for connecting with you. Then you can imagine disconnecting those cords. You need to do that anyway because you don't want to be overwhelmed by that energy in your daily life. This kind of work belongs in your private world.

Exercise 8

Stepping Into
Your Soulmate

You've called in your soulmate's essence to surround and touch you (exercise 1). This time, you get to step into your soulmate's essence, so you're actually submerged, sharing essences.

The best analogy to describe it is like a bath. You lower yourself into the bath water, bit by bit, to let yourself get accustomed to the temperature. Then, as the heat from the water penetrates your muscles, they relax and loosen, releasing the toxins and allowing you to absorb the relaxing warmth.

If you choose to actually use a bath to merge into your soulmate, feel free to do so. In that case, simply run the water and ask that your soulmate's essence imbue it. Then when you climb in, you will be sinking into them.

For several reasons, I chose not to use an actual bath for this exercise: Some people don't like baths, or they don't have bathtubs; it takes a certain amount of effort; and it's wet and messy. Using a chair or couch is simpler, and these are readily available to everyone.

This exercise is very simple, yet very powerful. I created it years ago and forgot about it until a friend reminded me of the remarkable success she had with it in manifesting her lover. It can be repeated often and, in fact, the more you do it, the stronger the connection it will create with your soulmate.

The process itself is not time-driven; it can take as long as thirty minutes or be as short as five minutes. What's important is not the length of the submersion, but the intensity and focus. So if you focus on your soulmate for five minutes, and you are totally engaged in feeling their essence caressing your skin, touching your heart, and embracing your body from the inside out, you will get as much benefit as a twenty-minute exercise.

You may not believe that anything is happening during the process, or you may feel nothing. Again, it is not necessary to sense something in order to postulate that it's happening. This admonition is particularly important if you are "dead below the neck," that is, you have turned off your awareness of feelings because they've been so painful. Yet they still exist and, eventually, you will become attuned to them.

As usual, do the process when things are quiet in your home, with no distractions. In fact, you can do it anywhere that's quiet since it is all done internally, and it does not need to take long.

Duration: Usually not longer than 15–20 minutes.

- Do the Grounding, Energy Clean-out, and Retrieving Your Energy exercises (page 38).

- Put on some evocative music. In this case, it might not be soft music, but something you really like. It might mean specific romantic music or music that makes you want to move in your soulmate's arms.

- Sit down in one chair across from an empty chair or couch. Take a few deep breaths in preparation.

- Call in your soulmate's essence and ask them to sit down in the empty chair. Doing so imbues that spot with their essence.

- When you're ready, stand up and walk over to them. Very slowly and mindfully, sit down into your soulmate. Let their essence surround and penetrate your body. Bathe in it. Inundate your-

self with your soulmate's essence. Feel it on
your skin, in your heart, in your mind. Imagine
they're whispering sweet nothings in your ear
as they hug you from the inside out.

- Imagine a ball of pink light surrounding you
  and your soulmate so that the two of you are
  enclosed by this radiant orb. This pink light lets
  your essences merge more intensely.

- If any doubts, fears, or worries come up, thank
  them; then imagine that they're bubbles floating
  off your body and popping into oblivion. Continue to do this visualization throughout the
  exercise whenever the voices recur. As each bub-
  ble departs, it leaves a little hole in your energy
  field where those fears and doubts were stuck.
  The light fills up those holes as well.

- Continue breathing, releasing the doubts, and
  wallowing in your soulmate's essence. Make the
  experience more intense, more enjoyable.

- When you feel complete, stand up, as if you were getting up from the bathtub, with the water pouring off you. Imagine your soulmate's essence being left behind on the seat. Let the pink light dissipate.

- Return to your seat. Thank your soulmate for coming. Let your soulmate's essence go home.

Exercise 9

The Beacon

The beacon is an unconscious mechanism inside your heart that's been set up to find you a particular kind of relationship. One way to visualize it is as a satellite dish that starts rotating whenever you meet someone. Here's how it works: Every time the beacon gets activated, it sends out signals, like a bat's echolocation sonar, searching for the person that matches its program. When its signals hit a possible mate's energy field or aura, that in turn activates the other person's beacon, which sends the requested information back to your beacon.

Another way to describe it is like two computers talking to each other via modem. They have to have a "handshake" (exchange of information) to establish that they can talk to each other. That's when a connection is made.

As soon as your beacon receives the signal back, it uses that information to determine whether that person has something in common with you, and how much. The more their particular qualities match your program, the more appealing that person will be to you than if they don't.

If your beacon broadcasts, "I'm looking for XYZ," and the other beacon replies, "I have ABZ," your beacon instantly dismisses that person ("too different") and moves on.

What happens when you run into someone whose beacon beams back "XYZ"? A match! Fireworks! Bells and whistles! You've found somebody that fits your criteria! You want to get to know them! That's when you begin gravitating toward that person to make the connection, knowing unconsciously that they are already attractive to you.

This whole sorting-out process takes a split second (far shorter than this explanation). And by now you've gotten it down to a science. It is literally as fast as glancing around the room at each person. In that moment, you reject or approve possible mates, all because of your beacon's say-so. You only know the results of its search—and it's completely unconscious.

That's why Jody unerringly chose the abuser, and Dave inevitably got involved with the same desperately needy type over and over again (different face and body, same problem).

How did this happen? When you first started activating your beacon, it relied on childhood family patterns to help you make sensible choices about lovers—"Is that the right lover or not?"—but with no real understanding of why you were attracted to them. Now those old patterns are set in your beacon, and it's still attracting that same kind of person. Now you don't really want them in your life. That's the problem.

As yet, your beacon can only find the kind of person it's programmed for, regardless of what you want. It is like the sorcerer's apprentice, a robot, doing its mindless task until you find the magic words to stop it. So far, you haven't had the ability or proper spell to do that.

It's time to give your sorcerer's apprentice a new spell, something more up-to-date that allows your beacon to adapt as you evolve. More importantly, this time you're going to expose the beacon to your soulmate's energy, so it will search for that.

You can reprogram the beacon yourself, or you can let your Higher Self do it. The easiest way to reconfigure your beacon is to replace it with a new mechanism altogether, something programmed for your soulmate. If you don't want to let it go, you can clean off the old one, bring it into the present, and ask that your soulmate come in and stamp their energy into the beacon.

When you turn on the beacon, it will start broadcasting that signal to attract that soulmate energy, whether it means one or several of them. Be prepared. You might have a very active social life!

Now take a moment to ask yourself: Do you have the ability and willingness to allow these new partners into your life once you start attracting them? Be honest with yourself. If the answer isn't an unequivocal YES, better do some release work fast! Otherwise, you might be overwhelmed and push your soulmate away, which you don't want to happen.

Once the beacon has been reconfigured to reflect you and your soulmate now, it will vibrate on a much higher frequency. You will start noticing changes on all levels—in the kinds of people you meet, in your family and friends, in your belief system—as you prepare for your soulmate.

Supplies: Sweetgrass or Nag Champa incense.

Duration: 30 minutes.

- Do the Grounding, Energy Clean-out, and Retrieving Your Energy exercises (page 38).

- Put on soft music. Burn some sweetgrass or Nag Champa incense to cleanse yourself. You want your energy to be as clear as possible.

- Call in your Higher Self. It will assist and guide you in removing and reprogramming your beacon.

- Take an escalator from your mind down to your heart (this is not your physical heart, but a symbolic one). That's where you will find your beacon. Take a look at it, or get a sense of what it's like. (If you can't see/sense/feel it, just imagine it's there.) This is what has been in charge of attracting your lovers into your life. Unless you're really attached to it, throw it out. Let your Higher Self bring in a new one.

- If you do want to hold on to the old beacon, ask your Higher Self to bring in a vat of golden liquid. Put the beacon into the vat to clean it off.

- Take out the beacon. Notice its condition. If it looks okay, it's functional. Otherwise, if it looks battered, or doesn't work, or makes obnoxious noises, or is otherwise unsuitable, throw it away. Ask your Higher Self to provide you with a newer, higher vibration model.

- Call in your soulmate. With your Higher Self holding the beacon, let your soulmate infuse the beacon with their essence so it will transmit a signal that searches for that vibration in the world. Here are some suggestions for doing that:

    Put the soulmate program into the beacon

    Have the soulmate essence actually stamp itself into the beacon, like an acid

    Replace the old attraction module with your soulmate module

    Embed an image of you and your soulmate happily being together in the beacon's transmitting mechanism

- Put the beacon, new or refurbished, back on the wall. Turn it on. It is sending out its signal, looking for your soulmate. Now that it's doing its job, get ready for your soulmate to show up!

Spinning

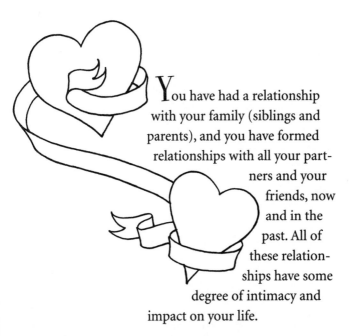

You have had a relationship with your family (siblings and parents), and you have formed relationships with all your partners and your friends, now and in the past. All of these relationships have some degree of intimacy and impact on your life.

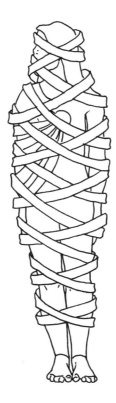

Past relationships, in the shape of cords,
may bind you in your soulmate search.

Unless you have done some kind of release work, each of these relationships remains with you in the form of cords that are attached to your heart. Depending on the complexity of the relationship, that cord may be wrapped around your body, so that it binds you.

Some part of your energy has been engaged with that particular part of your life, so it is not available to you. It means that you don't have all of your life force available. It's as though you have become compartmentalized.

How do you know? Think about an old lover or a family member, someone who causes you to have a strong emotional reaction. What kind of feeling do you get in your body? The stronger it is, the more energy you have wrapped up with them.

It's like a molehill and a mountain. The more you think about a problem, the more energy you throw at it, so a minor problem swells until it becomes a mountain of frozen energy. It only goes away when the problem is resolved. Suddenly you feel a rush as the energy gets released from the mountain; now it can return to your central pool of energy. (Remember the closet being cleaned—same idea.)

If you can't get over a person, or they remain in your thoughts, or you have a reaction to them (good or bad), they're still a part of your energy field, taking away some of your life force. Their cords have been wrapped around you, restricting your thoughts, feelings, and desires. By unwinding these cords, both you and the other person in this relationship can be disconnected emotionally and energetically.

Have you ever spun a pole that has been wound with string? As the pole spins, the string slackens and then spins away. That's what you will be doing in this exercise—spinning the bindings free, and then disconnecting them from you with help. Once that's done, you can take on your soulmate's essence.

The spinning is a two-way action: First, counterclockwise to release, and then clockwise to bring in—spinning away old relationships and spinning in your soulmate.

Your helpers this time will be from the angelic realm. The reason I recommend using the angels is that they can do the work of removing the cords you unwind without your ego or fear getting in the way. As you do the work, you may not want to release some of the cords because of your own fears or an old partner's needs. Leave the release work to the angels; they will do it impeccably, and with gentle detachment.

To begin, ask the angels to pick up the cords for each person who is wrapped around you. You may not have a very clear idea of who these people are. Some of you will need hundreds of angels for all the cords. Others will need just a few. It's unnecessary for you to know how many cords are attached to you. Just ask that as many angels help you as you need. They will unwind the cords as you spin.

You may want to remove only a few cords each time you do this exercise because you may feel a little naked without your mummy wrap. Your intent is important. Don't rush. Take your time with this work and do it at your comfortable pace.

Once you are free of the bindings, you will find yourself with a great deal more life-force energy. The more of yourself that you can claim, the more complete you are when you greet your soulmate.

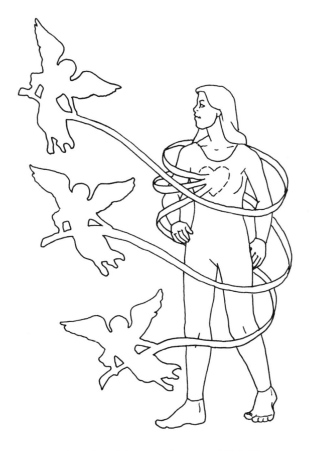

Angels helping to spin away old bindings.

Duration: 30 minutes.

- Do the Grounding, Energy Clean-out, and Retrieving Your Energy exercises (page 38).

- Stand in the middle of the room. Give yourself space to move, including wobbling space. Spinning can lead to a little bit of imbalance and staggering around.

- Imagine that each relationship you've had is a ribbon wound around your body. Call on an angel to find that end. You may get a sense of which person this cord connects to. Or you may deliberately say, "I am giving the angel the cord from my father/sister/brother/mother/lover (name them)." I recommend that you limit the number of cords that the angels take, at least the first time, from one to three, until you get accustomed to the experience.

- Spin counterclockwise slowly. You're not supposed to emulate a dervish; don't spin fast. I don't want you to lose your balance. You may be only able to spin a few turns. Rest for awhile, then continue. Keep turning until you feel that you've unwound the string. You may not feel that it's being unwound, or even that it's completely unwound, but your body will recognize it on some instinctual level. Stop when it seems right.

- When you've unwound the string, take your hand and actually pull its end out of your heart, like pulling a plug out of a socket. Then let the angel take the ribbon away. You may feel some reaction (other than dizziness), like relief, anger, sadness, or surprise; or memories may come up of people and events long past. That's a result of your energy returning to you.

- If you're game, repeat the procedure with a few more people. You can spin free of several relationships at a time.

- Now let a sunbeam come down through the top of your head. Let its golden light fill up all these spaces in your heart where those cords were attached, and then radiate through your aura. It helps readjust and realign all the energy that has been released into your body.

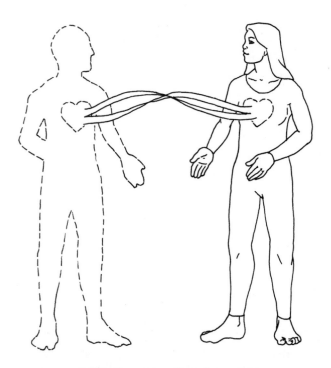

Calling in your soulmate's essence.

- Take a few deep breaths and bend over. Hang your head down for a few moments to release any excess energies. Then straighten up. This is a natural break between one segment and another and allows you to shift your vibration from letting go to calling in.

- Call in your soulmate's essence so they are standing across from you. Send a ribbon of love from your heart to their heart, and ask that they send a ribbon back to you.

- Then, spinning slowly clockwise, wind those ribbons around you, letting your body be wrapped in your soulmate's essence. Spin as long as you want. The more you spin, the more of your soulmate's essence is wrapped around you.

You may wish to repeat this whole exercise more than once. Although you may hope you've released all those people attached to you, you're likely to discover there are more underneath, hidden away, which will begin to be revealed as others are released.

Exercise 11

Angels and the Cosmic Cord

No set of exercises is complete without one that involves your most eager helpers and guides: Your angels. They, more than any other beings, are delighted to support you in manifesting your special soulmate relationship. After all, they have your best interests at heart, so what better thing to do than to let them help bring your soulmate to you? Their presence reminds you, whether you know it or not, that you are loved, that you are important, and that you are special. And, equally important, they are always available for help.

Since angels are transcendent beings, they have a different perspective on your life journey. They want the best for you. Yet that might mean watching you endure painful experiences that are necessary for your growth, or struggle to release karmic debts or traumas. Nevertheless, their angelic love is there, comforting and safe and uplifting.

How do you use angels to your best ability, to give you what you want and to help you manifest your desires joyously and easily?

You ask directly for their aid. You can call on them to help you in a specific situation, or you can ask for general help, or, in this case, you can ask them to bring in your soulmate. But you also must do your part, as well; you must commit yourself to the quest, whatever it brings. For this exercise, you are going to ask the angels for help with your cosmic cord.

A cosmic cord is a special ribbon of energy connecting two people's hearts, and it flows from the angels into both your hearts. It's a transcendent blessing given to you by the angels.

Energy cords are usually attached to us in particular chakras from other people, whether they are our parents, lovers, children, friends, coworkers, bosses, religious figures, and so on. These energy cords get in your way and inhibit your growth by siphoning away your energy. And you do the same with other people as well.

Before you can activate your cosmic cord, you need to remove as many of these energy cords as you can (see exercise 10), disconnecting yourself from others but leaving your own energy intact. Once they are removed, you can accept cosmic cords that provide you with a continuous current of joy and love.

Both you and your soulmate will be linked by a cosmic cord of angelic love. It's yet another way to magnetize the two of you together, as long as it is in the highest good of you and your soulmate.

When you ask the angels to bring that cosmic cord from them to you and your soulmate, they also shower you both with their benison or blessing.

You might imagine the angels standing at the top of an angle, beaming out the cosmic cord to both of you, and then, once you two are attached to it, bringing a ring of light around you that shrinks until you two are next to each other.

Duration: Up to 30 minutes.

- Do the Grounding, Energy Clean-out, and Retrieving Your Energy exercises (page 38). Put on comforting music and close your eyes.

- Remove the cords from your chakras (see exercise 10). Think of them as plugs at the end of retractable cords that are being pulled out of sockets in your chakra. When they are released, they zip home to their owners. Do this with each chakra (back and front; refer to figure on page 85). You can't put in a cosmic cord with all that other interference.

- Call on the angels of love. Imagine yourself like a bowl ready to be filled with angelic love.

- Let the angels send cosmic cords down to both you and your soulmate. This is pure angelic love being given to you. It creates a channel through which their love is pouring down into your heart. The same thing is being done with your soulmate.

- Now it's your turn. Focus a beam of love out of your heart into your soulmate's heart, and, of course, imagine that they are doing the same thing toward you, so that there are two beams of love, one from each heart. You are involved in three actions here: You're beaming love to your soulmate, your soulmate is beaming love to you, and your angels are beaming love to the both of you.

- Let the angels put a ring of light around you both. Gradually that ring shrinks, slowly, slowly, until you and your soulmate are energetically nose to nose with each other, no longer apart on this spiritual plane, but connected.

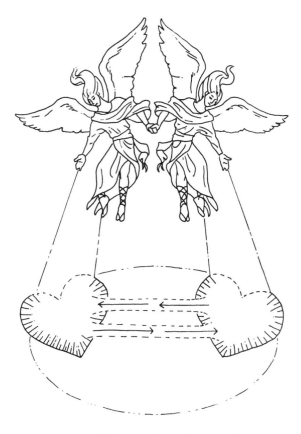

Angels and the cosmic cords connecting
you and your soulmate.

- Remain inside that angelic circle for a few moments, feeling the current of love flowing between all of you.

- Then, when you're ready, open your eyes and come back to the room.

You can repeat this exercise any time. This is a safe one to use in getting accustomed to your soulmate's energy.

Exercise 12

Candle Burning

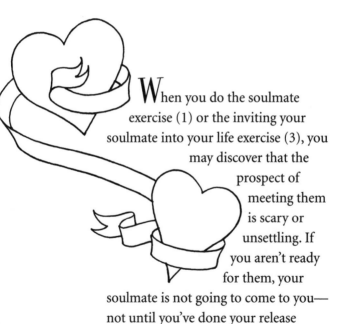

When you do the soulmate
exercise (1) or the inviting your
soulmate into your life exercise (3), you
may discover that the
prospect of
meeting them
is scary or
unsettling. If
you aren't ready
for them, your
soulmate is not going to come to you—
not until you've done your release

work and created that receptiveness inside. One way to do that is with candle burning in ritual, in meditation, and in prayer.

The candle acts as a focus for your energies, your will, your desire, your hope. In this exercise, you will be using first one colored candle, then another. As the first candle burns, it works to release old programs, energies, and vibrations. Then the second candle focuses on attracting your soulmate.

It's important to burn the color that fits a particular purpose, since different colors denote different desires or energies; and each color has its own vibrations.

Love candles are pink (which is for affinity/love).

Attraction candles are red.

Release candles are black or white.

Before going any further, let me explain the difference between attraction and love (they are not the same). Attraction is something you feel toward someone, anyone. It often has a strong element of sexuality attached to it. In fact, you can have attraction without emotional engagement. Love, on the other hand, is a heart feeling you share with a particular person, preferably your soulmate. If you want to attract someone (anyone), burning a red candle is fine. For your soulmate, use a pink love candle.

A number of companies make candles for specific purposes (Prosperity, Sacred Space, Meditation, Love, Attraction, and so on). These candles have been prepared with specific herbs and minerals that enhance their particular purpose. The idea is that as the candle burns, it imbues the area with the energy of prosperity, for example, so that it magnetizes the quality or energy to you.

For your work, I suggest you not use one of these candles until the end of the exercise, once the old programs have been burned out and you have become attuned to your soulmate's energy. At that point, it will have more of an impact because you will be more open and receptive to its energies.

Some metaphysical stores "dress" candles with appropriate energies and symbols. These are not like the professional candles because you buy the particular color of candle and then let them be prepared for you. Those may be used during any part of this candle burning, and will enhance your focus.

Supplies: A black or white release candle and a pink love candle, at least 6" high and 1–2" wide, not little skinny ones. Optional: A professionally made attraction or love candle. Also love oil.

Duration: 30 minutes, at first.

- Do the Grounding, Energy Clean-out, and Retrieving Your Energy exercises (page 38).

- Put on some evocative music (whatever appeals to you).

- Light the release candle. Let it burn for a few moments. Then, as you watch the candle flickering, say, "I am burning all that stands in my way of finding my soulmate." Imagine all the blocks, obstacles, and fears that are keeping you from your soulmate being burned out of your heart chakra.

- Take your hands and actually grab at the air about two to three inches in front of your heart (fourth) chakra, as if you were pulling out invisible spaghetti or strands of seaweed that were stuck on your heart and chest. This is the stuff

that's blocking you from your soulmate. Throw
this imaginary kelp into the candle flame and let
it burn.

- Repeat the words and action in your third chakra
(stomach/solar plexus); then at your genital area
(second chakra), and the base of your spine (first
chakra). Then clean out your throat (fifth
chakra), your brow (sixth chakra), and top
of your head (seventh chakra). (See figure,
page 85.)

- Don't neglect the back of your body (chakras
have two ends). Clean them out as well.

- Continue this grabbing/throwing away motion
at each chakra until you feel you are pretty clean.
It will take about 10–15 minutes if you've rarely
done this kind of clean-out, less once you've
become more adept at it (and cleaner).

- Blow out the release candle.

- Allow a beam of sunlight to flow through you
and fill all those places that have been emptied.

This golden light also helps you realign your inner vibrations. Take a deep, cleansing breath.

- Light the pink candle.

- Say, "I'm lighting this candle to attract my soulmate. As this candle burns, I open to my soulmate."

- Call in your soulmate's essence. Imagine them touching your whole body, from your head, neck, fingers, chest, shoulders, and so on. Take some time to really get into this experience (up to 10 minutes). It can be as pleasurable as you wish. (You may want to use the protocol in exercise 7.)

- If you have an attraction or love candle, now is the time to light it. Let it burn until it is gone.

It is recommended that you do this process three to five more times (on different days). There's always more cleaning to do, and it makes the calling stronger.

Exercise 13

The Doll

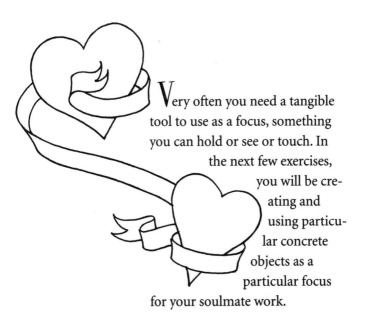

Very often you need a tangible tool to use as a focus, something you can hold or see or touch. In the next few exercises, you will be creating and using particular concrete objects as a particular focus for your soulmate work.

In this exercise, you're going to use a doll-like form, no more than eight inches tall and made out of any kind of natural material (fabric, wood, clay, but *not* plastic). Sometimes you can get an anonymous humanoid form from a craft store, or you can make it yourself out of some material. It needs to be material that lasts, since you will be keeping it for some time.

This doll will be given certain attributes. In a way, it's like a voodoo doll, but instead of sticking pins in it, you're going to fill it with the qualities of your soulmate.

Before you start, remember that your soulmate is not your ideal mate. Your ideal mate is a construct of your mind, an amalgam of qualities and beliefs that you think you want. It may (and often does) have nothing whatsoever to do with the reality of your soulmate (see exercise 2).

For example, your ideal mate may be neat as a pin, while your soulmate, it turns out, is a mess (though hopefully not as bad as Oscar in *The Odd Couple*). If you put the qualities you want from your ideal mate in this doll, that's what you'll get—not your soulmate.

But wait a minute! How do I know what my soulmate is like, you're asking? How can I put any qualities in this doll?

Well, there are a few that are requisite, no matter what kind of person they are: Loving, caring, supportive, intelligent, humorous, joyful.

If you don't believe you deserve these qualities in your relationship (and many people don't), you are wrong! Other qualities you should expect from your soulmate are: Compatibility, being on the same wavelength, having similar spiritual values (in other words, a fundamentalist and an atheist together are hardly conducive to harmony), a desire to be with you (which they should anyway, they're your soulmate!), understanding you, and being each other's best friend. That's the least you should expect in any relationship, especially with your soulmate.

Notice that I'm not focusing on particular character traits like "neatness," but rather essential qualities that are important for any good relationship.

Until you meet them, you may not know their height, ethnicity, race, hair color, and so on, but as you continue touching your soulmate's essence, you may get "hits" on what feels right to you. Suddenly, you'll get an intuition about the color blue, or their height, or Reese's Pieces (and you're not a Reese's Pieces addict, so it must be their passion). Those are things you can add to your doll. You may be surprised at the number and kind of hits you get as you do this exercise.

Before you start, I suggest you burn some incense to clear the air and put you into a receptive mind set, and to call in your guidance. I recommend a light sweet stick incense like Nag Champa, which you can buy at most alternative stores or wherever they carry Indian imports.

Supplies: A small humanoid figure; crayons, fine-line magic markers, or colored pens in several bright colors; small multicolored papers or fabrics (red and pink especially); glue; pins; tape; pink, red, white, and gold ribbons in various lengths; scissors; beads, feathers or other decorations; Nag Champa incense.

Duration: 1 hour maximum.

- Gather all your supplies together.

- Find your sacred quiet space in your home or out in nature, where you won't be disturbed. It will be difficult to do this process well if there are distractions.

- If you can, put on some music, something that will enhance your mood and concentration but not detract from it (not loud, jangly music—rap and rock are out). After all, you're trying to evoke a romantic mood to call in your soulmate.

- Do the Grounding, Energy Clean-out, and Retrieving Your Energy exercises (page 38).

- Light the incense and pass it in a circle around your work area. Then pass the doll through the smoke to clean out all the old energies it still may hold. You want to put your own energies into it.

- If your doll does not have a face, draw it in with your magic markers or pens. Make it as detailed or abstract as you feel comfortable doing.

- Call in your soulmate's essence (exercise 1). Take a moment or two to sense and hold that essence in your mind and body.

Supplies for making a love doll.

- In a clear voice, state what you're doing: "I am asking that the essence of my soulmate manifest in this doll." Then let that essence flow into your doll.

- Take a piece of red or pink paper or fabric. Cut out a heart and write on it, "My soulmate loves me." Imagine your soulmate's energy imbuing this heart. Stick it on the doll's chest using glue, pins, tape, or a ribbon.

- Make another heart and stick it right on top of the first one. This one says, "I love my soulmate." Let your energy imbue that heart.

- Take a piece of paper or fabric. Write down the qualities of your soulmate. You may use a single piece of paper for each quality, or list them all on one sheet. Start with the qualities you deserve from any relationship, no matter who it is: Loving, caring, supportive, intelligent, humorous, joyous, and so on. You may also receive intuitions about your soulmate's other qualities or traits as you call on their essence; for example, something like their favorite color. Let your soul-mate's energy pour over these qualities.

- Attach these qualities to the doll in whatever manner you like. Be creative. Use your imagination and your sense of what you and your soul-mate would like. Here are some suggestions:

  Staple or glue them to a ribbon, and tie the ribbon around the body

  Glue or tape them to the body and wrap the ribbon around the body

  Write them on the doll itself with the magic marker or pen if it's cloth

  Write them on little hearts and stick them on so the doll is covered with them

  Sew them on

- As you do the last step, say something like, "I am filling this doll with our combined essences so that it is a magnet for us both. We now have a true connection here." At the same time, imagine

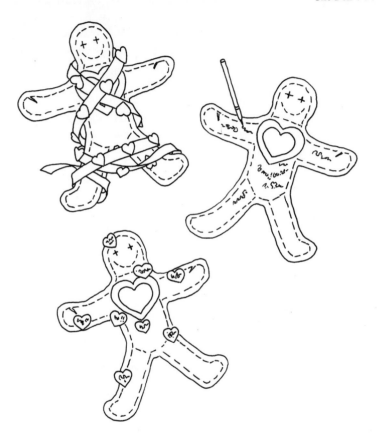

Examples of love dolls.

that you are imbuing the doll with your energy and your soulmate's. Repeat that sentence until you have completely finished putting on the hearts.

- You have created a tangible in-the-world object. Now say, "I am making my soulmate relationship as tangible as this doll, and soon he/she will be here in actuality—as long as this relationship is for our highest good."

- Put the doll on your altar or someplace where you can see and touch it or hold it. Each time, in fact, that you do that, you reinforce the connection with your soulmate.

- When your soulmate arrives, you can bury or burn this doll (and all your other talismans). You may want to turn it into a ceremony that the two of you perform together as a reminder of how these objects helped bring you together.

Exercise 14

The Collage of
Your Relationship

Like the doll, you are going to
create a tangible object for your focus,
but this one is in two dimensions. Your
soulmate collage is not
simply an interest-
ing picture. Its
purpose is to
convey the feeling
sense of your
relationship-to-be.
What is the kind of relationship
you want to build? How do you

159

feel about it and your soulmate? Those are the questions your collage will address.

Your relationship starts with the shape of the picture you make. Most collages are a collection of pictures glued onto a backing, usually rectangular. Yours will be whatever is right for this relationship. That shapes and enhances the whole process and defines the relationship-to-be.

What form is it going to be? A heart? An oval or a ring? A circle or a square? Or a spiral? A spiral has the dynamic of movement. A circle and a square describe perfection; one is dynamic, the other static. Some people choose the infinity symbol, the lying-down figure eight, which is appropriate because your soulmate and you have been around for an infinite number of lifetimes. Or you can simply use the typical rectangle.

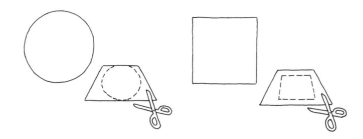

By creating this collage around a particular form, with its inherent set of qualities, it also affects you as well, particularly if it portrays qualities you feel you lack. *This is a very important point.* The collage magnetizes or accentuates certain positive patterns or feelings that you don't acknowledge in yourself. That will create a tension or discomfort within you.

For example, suppose you have had relationships that were abusive, neglectful, or unfulfilling. They reflect your old childhood patterns that have recurred over and over in your relationships.

Your collage should *not* reflect that abuse or neglect, but rather express your desire for love, support, and joy. But you may feel uncomfortable with, or distrustful of, those feelings—or even believe you don't deserve them. That means every time you look at the collage, with its

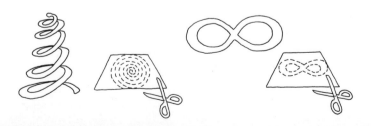

loving images, the patterns in you that cause you to feel unworthy of having this love are going to be triggered.

You may hear voices telling you that you don't deserve love like this. Or you may get other negative messages, like, "You're not lovable." Once you begin to hear them, it becomes possible to confront them and begin to dismantle them (good riddance!). (See exercise 4 for a more in-depth discussion of how to remove patterns.)

As you keep looking at this collage and dealing with the negative messages that keep arising, you can really open to the joy and love expressed in your picture.

Supplies: Various magazines; glue; some kind of backing, like cardboard; colored paper or fabric to glue on the cardboard; scissors; decorative items you'd like to add (beads, feathers, and so on).

Duration: 1 hour maximum.

- Before you begin, collect all the ingredients for your collage, either from your own supplies or bought from stores. Thrift stores are a good place to get all kinds of magazines. That may mean spending a few hours or days gathering them in advance.

- Find a place to work on your collage undisturbed.

- Do the Grounding, Energy Clean-out, and Retrieving Your Energy exercises (page 38).

- Put on some evocative music. In this case, it might not be soft music, but something you really like, which will help imbue your collage with your energy.

- Call in your Higher Self or an angel for input and guidance.

- Call in your soulmate essence (exercise 1).

- What is the shape that expresses how you want your soulmate relationship to be? Let your mind relax so you can hear the answer. You might ask your Higher Self for a suggestion. When you have received an impression, cut out the background. That's why cardboard is probably best.

You might even want to use paper; then after the collage is finished, you can glue it on a stiff backing. If you get no particular impression, choose a shape that you like or that feels harmonious to you. Enjoyment is a desirable quality in any soulmate work, particularly a collage.

- Ask your soulmate to help you choose what pictures belong on this collage. Keep in mind the qualities of the relationship you want to include. What are the qualities you'd like in your love? (For example: love, enjoyment, touching, affection, respect, humor, equality.) How do you want to express them in your relationship?

- Feel those pictures you are choosing. If there are people laughing, tune into your own sense of humor and joy when you are with your soulmate. If you see loving people, touch the loving center within you, and feel or imagine the love between you and your soulmate.

- Make your collage. Create a picture of the kind of relationship you intend to have with your soulmate.

- When you feel like you have included all you need in your picture, stop. Do not overembellish your collage, even if you only use a few pictures or items. The only important criterion is that they are the right items.

- When you have finished your collage, put it on the wall in a special place where you can contemplate it every day to remind yourself of the relationship you want (like on or around your altar). The more you do that, the more likely you will be to release those internal blocks, and then magnetize your soulmate to you.

The Shield

The shield is similar to a collage in that it's two-dimensional, but it has a different focus and appearance. It is a spiritual picture of you and your soulmate together. In the collage, you were asked to express the desired relationship through the shape of the picture you created.

With the shield, you tune into the spiritual connection you have with yourself, your soulmate, and the energies that will be helping to manifest your relationship.

You definitely don't want to create a shield that is simply pretty. Art is not the goal. It's manifestation, spiritual manifestation. Your shield is not a picture. It is a symbolic vision. You imbue a shield not with desire, but with a spiritual blessing—so that what you create has balance and rightness. That means that instead of pictures, you will be using symbolic objects that you have bought or collected.

Each spirit object has (or should have) a particular spiritual resonance. As a whole, they enhance the harmony and purpose of the shield. These objects will not be glued or stuck in a pattern that just creates a pleasing picture, nor will they go on haphazardly; they create a spiritually complete whole. They are not just a group of pictures that express love and other qualities. (Put those in your collage.)

There are several ways to create a shield.

If you were making a traditional Native American shield, you would be chanting and fasting and preparing yourself. You might spend time on a vision quest, and you'd pay attention to your dreams. Then you would ask for a vision of the symbols that belong on your shield. You would find a willow branch, curve it into a circle, and tie it with rawhide; then you would stretch and tie deer hide over it. Once it was ready, you would paint your symbols on your shield.

In this day and age, most people don't have the time, energy, or resources for such an undertaking. There is nothing wrong with the spiritual preparation of meditation, dream work, visions, and fasts. Those are all excellent preparatory steps. But unlike the Native Americans who may do them over many days, often isolated in the wilderness, you may want to do a meditation or mini-journey that lasts an hour or so over a period of several days, with or without fasting during that time. It is your decision.

Just like with the collage, you should not have a set design in mind. Let it flow from your Higher Self, your unconscious, and your soulmate. Then put your vision or concept into the form of your shield.

For your materials you may use somewhat more modern substitutes that can be obtained at local stores, like an embroidery hoop and fabric. It's easy to create your shield; just cut out the proper-sized fabric, pop it between the two pieces of the hoop, and you have an easy surface to decorate in two or three dimensions.

Then you can use the fabric paint to create the symbols and add the decorations you feel are appropriate, like feathers, beads, little trinkets (you can find some wonderful ones at bead stores), pictures, glitter, ribbon—whatever your mind can conceive.

Don't expect your shield to necessarily look pretty. This is not its purpose. It is designed for power: The power to manifest your soulmate. Your symbols also have their own inherent strength. Putting them together enhances and combines those powers. In fact, after you are done, it may not look particularly attractive or good-looking, but it will, hopefully, be strong.

This is a spiritual construct, and the more in tune it is with the highest levels of your spirit, the more powerful the energies that are entwined with it.

Choose the proper time to create your shield, a particular time of day or month that adds psychic strength to your work. That means doing it during the waxing moon (which symbolizes increase), not the waning moon (which represents letting go). You most definitely don't want to let go. You also want to do it preferably on a Friday, which is the day of Aphrodite/Venus (love), although Monday (emotion) is also acceptable.

What kinds of symbols do you want to use? That's up to you. Each of us has specific symbols that have meaning for us. When you do a meditation and you see particular symbols, those are appropriate for you to put on your shield.

What kinds of symbols work? Laura's soulmate shield may be described as follows: On it are hearts (of course) all around the embroidery hoop; also a bow, which she describes as tying the two of them together, overseen by the Angel of Love, which she painted in the background with the fabric paint and sprinkled with glitter. Then she added little glitter angels, as well as lightning bolts (for being zapped with love) and big smiles and cats (she's a cat person and her soulmate better be, too!).

Beth created seven different shields, each one depicting seven phases of her spiritual journey with her soulmate, which she hung around her bedroom. Each one had its own impact, but as a whole, they were very intense. Needless to say, her soulmate couldn't help but appear!

Adam used a small number of crystals that he stuck around the edge of the embroidery hoop. As a background, he used a large lace doily, which he decorated with more crystals and various objects, many of which he created himself, such as figurines of him and his soulmate.

The limits of shield creation are your own imagination, your Higher Self's suggestions, and your soulmate's essence—as long as the symbolism enhances the total vision, which is manifesting your soulmate.

Supplies: Embroidery hoop; plain fabric, like muslin or other colored cotton cloth if you want to paint on it; lace or other kinds of fabric, if that is what your vision calls for; fabric paints; glitter; beads; feathers; seeds; pictures; symbols of various sorts that have spiritual meaning to you; copal, sage, or sweetgrass for incense; glue; tape; ribbons; scissors; decorations.

Duration: 1 hour.

- Before you begin, collect all the ingredients for your shield. That may mean spending a few hours or days gathering them in advance. As you collect them, either from your personal effects or at stores, ask your Higher Self for spiritual guidance in choosing the right items to give the most intensity to the shield. Also, ask that your soulmate's essence send you visions or sensations of particular items that they would like to see represented as well. You might also have dreams that tell you what objects to use.

- Prepare yourself with a ritual bath to wash away the old and open yourself to the new.

- Light the copal, sage, or sweetgrass, and cense your area. Make sure it stays burning throughout your process.

- Do the Grounding, Energy Clean-out, and Retrieving Your Energy exercises (page 38). Put on some evocative music. In this case, you might want to stay with the Native American motif and use flute or drumming music.

- Meditate for about 15 minutes. At the beginning of this meditation, announce that you are ready to create your soulmate shield, and ask to see any symbols that would be most appropriate on it.

- Aloud, call on your Higher Self, an angel, Mother/Father God, your power animal, or any other higher beings that you work with to come and lend their power, wisdom, and insight to your work. Ask that they help you create the spirit of your relationship on this shield.

- Call in your soulmate's essence.

- Create the shield. When you feel that it is complete, no matter how many objects you have placed on it, stop. Do not overembellish your shield, even if you only put on a few objects. The only important criterion is that

they are the right ones. Too much stuff
dilutes its impact.

- When you have finished your shield, put it on
  the wall in a special place where you can contemplate it every day to remind yourself of the relationship you want (i.e., on or around your altar).
  The more you do that, the more likely you will
  be to magnetize them to you.

- You may go back later and add more objects, if
  you feel that's appropriate, particularly if you
  find something that just has to go on your shield.

Exercise 16

The Talisman

A talisman is another kind of tangible object that you imbue with the energy of your soulmate. In this exercise, we're going to learn the ritual for consecrating a soulmate talisman. First, you need to select something that you'd like to designate as a talisman. It may be as simple as a rock or stone, or a small picture, a crystal, a statuette, jewelry—as long as it's an item that has spiritual significance for you. It needs to be small because you want to carry it with you.

How do you pick a talisman? It is often something that appeals to you esthetically or emotionally. It helps if you feel some kind of reaction to it (in this case, something like love or good will). Your talisman should embody the qualities that fit its purpose. For example, if you're going to make a money talisman, you will probably use coins.

For a love talisman, you want something that connotes love. Some suggestions are things like the Irish claddagh heart ring, hearts of various shapes (like a crystal heart), a Welsh love spoon, or a love angel. There are all kinds of possibilities; the limits are your imagination. You do want something that's unbreakable, though, as a broken talisman evokes unfortunate connotations.

Next, your talisman should not be something you've used for another purpose (i.e, as another talisman). You want it to be special for this purpose alone. Choose something unique and new for your soulmate. After all, this work is to create a new relationship, not recycle an old pattern.

Once you have chosen your talismanic object, you must clean out the old energies that are still stuck in it before you can infuse it with your soulmate's and your energies. There are several ways to do that. I will describe only two, both of which are effective.

Wash it in sea water to remove the old energy. (If you don't live near an ocean, use sea salt in water.) If it's something like paper or fabric, the salt water might damage the object, so use this method for sturdy objects only.

A simpler and cleaner method is to imagine the object is filled with golden light that infuses every cell and dissolves all the old energies, letting them drain down into the earth for recycling. Repeat it as often as you need until you are sure the object is clean.

Either way you choose, once you've done this preparatory cleansing, you're ready to infuse it with soulmate energies.

Supplies: Love incense; red or pink paper; talisman; love oil; a pink candle; a cup of salt water; a plate of dirt; a small red or pink fabric pouch; red or gold ribbons. (The love incense and love oil can be bought at metaphysical stores or botanicas [herb stores]. See the list of resources at the back of this book.)

Duration: 30–45 minutes.

- Do the Grounding, Energy Clean-out, and Retrieving Your Energy exercises (page 38).

- Call in your Higher Self, angels, and any other higher beings to assist at this consecration.

- Call in your soulmate's essence.

- Burn the love incense.

- Take a piece of the pink or red paper large enough to wrap your talisman in. On it, write "My soulmate is my true love" (or similar words).

- Pick up your talisman. Anoint it with the love oil. (If it is something that stains, like paper, anoint it in an unobtrusive place.)

- Say, "My soulmate's love for me is in this talisman. This talisman is a beacon to bring my soulmate to me through (name the element: air, fire, water, earth)." Imagine your soulmate's energy flowing into this object.

- Say, "I infuse this talisman with my energy," and imagine that happening.

- Say, "Let my soulmate come to me."

- Repeat the preceding three steps as you consecrate the talisman with the four elements:

  Air (incense)

  Fire (candle—do it fast)

  Water (daub some on in an area that won't be stained)

  Earth (daub some dirt in an area that won't be marred)

- Concentrate on your soulmate's energy vibrating through this talisman.

- Once it's consecrated, just hold the talisman in your hand and imagine that it's pulsating with your mingled energies.

- Take the paper and wrap it around the talisman. Put it in the little pouch and tie it closed with the ribbon. Make sure the ribbon is secure.

- You may keep the talisman either on your altar or with you. Some people say that it's better to have it with you all the time. I personally have found that having it on the altar is enough for me.

The Flowering Plant

Planting a tree or plant is a powerful symbol of commitment.
It's actually feeding and expressing the
development of that con-
nection between
you two. For
example, let's
say you buy
yourself a rose-
bush and put it
into the ground. You water
and weed it, you talk to it and you

give it love, and it grows. It puts out buds, and then it's in bloom. Using this normal process of flowering, if you have chosen this rose as a symbol of your upcoming relationship, it creates a mystical bond between you and your soulmate.

Some people use a tree. I personally think that, once your lover has arrived, you two can get a tree and plant it together as a symbol of your love. Of course, that only works if you have an available yard.

If you're living in a condo or an apartment, you'd be better off with something in a movable pot. You want something that you can put on your altar, or wherever you keep your soulmate objects.

For this exercise, I want you to choose a plant that has flowers. Don't get a vine or a green plant like a scheffleria or ficus. A flowering plant symbolizes what your relationship is going to be doing.

Choose a flowering plant that gives you a good feeling. Roses have that feeling for many people, myself included. They are very popular because they have a lot of love symbolism attached to them. The right flowering plant has some meaning to you; when you look at it, your heart is filled with joy. Freesias, particularly, do that for me.

Another criterion for choosing a plant is that it has meaning for you. If it doesn't have meaning, what's the point of it? You might think, "Oh, I'm just going to get any old plant." No, no! Flowers come in so many colors; choose the one with the right vibration for you.

It would be nice if this plant were flowering or at least budding at the time you do your activation. As it grows and flowers, that's what will happen with your relationship.

Let's talk about a problem that I'm sure a number of you are concerned about: The plant dies. Is your love ruined?! Let's face it, no matter how hard some people work, they're never going to get a plant to live or thrive. It's not that your soulmate connection and your life force weren't strong enough to help the plant grow. It's that you and plants don't mix.

If you have a black thumb, don't do this exercise. You don't want to feel like you've jinxed your process (you haven't, but you might feel that way).

Suppose the plant just sits there, doing nothing. It may have some real problems, like it doesn't like the sun, or the shade, or the atmosphere, or your living space. Talk to it. Find out what it wants. (Yes, you can intuitively sense if a plant is happy, and even what it needs). I know this from experience. My plants just sat there and didn't die, and didn't grow. Finally I meditated on what they wanted, and I sensed they needed attention. That's when I started talking to the plants, telling them how much I liked them, and they responded quite nicely.

This exercise has two distinct segments.

Part I

Supplies: Plant; dirt or clean compost; spring water; mylar confetti (hearts, angels, dots, and so on); grain (corn, rice); patchouli, jasmine, or love incense (which you can get at a metaphysical store).

Duration: 30 minutes.

- Do the Grounding, Energy Clean-out, and Retrieving Your Energy exercises (page 38).

- Put on some evocative music. In this case, it might not be soft music, but something you really like, which will help imbue the plant with your energy.

- Call in your Higher Self or an angel for input and guidance.

- Call in your soulmate essence (exercise 1).

- Holding the plant in your hands, call in your soulmate's essence. Then imagine your soulmate putting their hands around the plant as well, so it is being held by both of you.

- Ask your Higher Self, angels, or guardian angel to put their hands around both of yours and imbue this plant with their blessing. Even if you do not sense anything happening, do it anyway. Postulating that it happens is as important as it happening. Allow yourself to be open to the process. The more intense the connection to the plant, the more energy you can put into the plant. As the plant absorbs this energy, it's going to feel loved and nurtured.

- Take the dirt and sprinkle it lightly around the plant, saying, "This dirt is the strength, solidity, and longevity of the enduring earth. It symbolizes the strength and endurance of our love." Avoid words like "eternity" and "forever" because they can come back and bite you.

- Pick up the spring water (nothing from the tap). You need plain water, not bubbly water. Pour it into the plant, saying, "This water nurtures this plant as our love nurtures us."

- Now pick up the mylar confetti. Sprinkle them around the pot while saying, "My soulmate and I put these hearts, et cetera, into the soil as a symbol of our growing and flowering love."

- Then take the grains. Toss them into the dirt, saying, "These symbolize our love growing, burgeoning, flowering."

- Now cense the plants with your incense.

- Once you've completed this little ceremony, put your plant on your altar or wherever it is most happy (sun, shade).

Part II

- Talk to your plant. A lot. Every day.

- As you do, call in your soulmate's energy so the two of you can talk to the plant together. When you talk to the plant, you're really talking to your soulmate through the plant. "My soulmate, I'm talking to you. As this plant is growing, as it's flowering and evolving, it's expressing the love and connection between us."

- Meanwhile, the plant starts doing positive things, like growing and flowering. A plant really and truly wants to be loved. It wants to be nurtured, it wants to feel your attention on it. Talking to it is very beneficial.

- After a month you can plant it into the ground outside, if possible, or leave it in its favorite spot.

Weaving a Calling

In a calling, you are using your thoughts, intent, and will to manifest what you need. It is a shamanic process, using Native American motifs and symbols. There are three distinct parts to this process—finding the supplies, weaving the object, and putting the object into the earth.

The most important thing with a calling is focus. The more strongly you focus on your soulmate and the desire to meet them as you weave your calling, the stronger it will be.

I learned about this exercise in a class on shamanism many years ago. It was spectacularly successful for me the first time I did it. My calling manifested in five days!

Unlike some of your other creations, this is not great art. It's a primitive weaving in which you create whatever feels right for you. Its purpose isn't decoration, it's manifestation, and that's what provides the power. Every single item on it has your energy, with meaning for you and you alone. That's why your concentration and focus are so significant.

Part I

- A few days before you do the calling, you need to gather your supplies. To do that, spend time walking in nature for about an hour, meditating, relaxing, and opening yourself to the world around you.

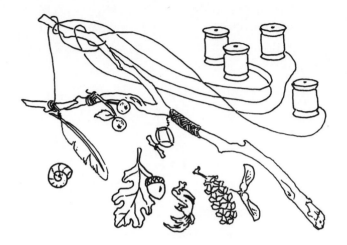

A weaving in progress.

- As you stroll along, pick up any natural objects that call to you, things that are not perishable that you can weave into your calling, like twigs, leaves, pine cones, buds, fruits, feathers, and so on. You don't want to use flowers that will wilt, unless they can be dried. Collect at least one or two every day.

- You also need to find a stick or branch to use as the frame for your weaving. It would be good if this stick had some personality, something with curves, with life, with intrigue.

- Store them all in a safe place, preferably somewhere near your altar, until you're ready.

Part II

- On the fifth or sixth day after you began collecting your objects, it's time for you to weave your calling. When I wove mine, I meditated beforehand for ten minutes, letting the image form before weaving it onto my branch.

- Once you've planted your calling, you must put it out of your mind. Forget about it. If you find yourself recalling it, push it out of your mind. The more you dwell on it, the more you hold onto the calling instead of letting it do its job. It's like holding on to your lover so they can't go do their work.

Supplies: Copal, sage, or sweetgrass (use native incenses rather than East Indian or resin incenses); colored yarn or threads of red, yellow, green, blue, white, and black (these are the Native American representations for the four directions, earth, and sky); the natural objects that you've collected on your walks. You may also want to include some beads, feathers, trinkets, colored paper, or other symbolic objects, but emphasize the found objects.

Duration: 1 hour.

- Gather all your supplies together on a surface, either on the floor or on a table. Be sure no one is around to disturb you.

- Do the Grounding, Energy Clean-out, and Retrieving Your Energy exercises (page 38).

- Put on some music. Native flute music will be very harmonious with your work. Don't use drumming music, which evokes a different kind of energy than you want here.

- Light your incense. Copal is a resin incense, so it will need a charcoal. Sweetgrass and sage burn on their own. Let them burn throughout the whole exercise.

- Call in your Higher Self for wisdom and guidance in this exercise.

- Call in your soulmate's essence.

- Close your eyes and ask your Higher Self for help in attracting your soulmate (if it's in alignment with your highest good). From now on, just accept that your Higher Self is taking charge of this process and guiding your hand. Let your mind relax so you can get in tune with the kind of weaving you want to create, which will create your calling. You may get an image, or you may not.

- Create your weaving on the branch. Remember to leave one end free to go into the ground. Don't necessarily stick with a preconceived notion of what you were going to weave or how you were going to structure it. In fact, you may just end up tying things onto the branch instead of formally "weaving" anything.

- As you create your weaving, imagine your soulmate's essence beside you—who they are, what they are like, how they are connected with you. Weave your soulmate's energy into this calling, and your own as well. You may even talk to your soulmate as you work (aloud or silently). You will see the object taking shape in front of you.

- When you feel that you are finished, no matter how much you've done, stop. Maybe you haven't used all your objects. That's okay. If it's right, that's what's important.

Part III

This is where you plant the branch into the earth so that the earth spirits can focus on the calling. Once you've made your object, give yourself a day or so to let the weaving absorb all the energy. Then you can plant it somewhere in nature, preferably where it won't be disturbed (although that's becoming harder and harder to find). Backyards, although practical, may not be the most ideal places because children, curious friends, and pets may dig up your weaving.

You may have to drive to various places until you find someplace that feels right. When I found the right place for my weaving and I planted it into the earth, it was like the earth sucked it in. I could feel the intensity; it was amazing. So was the speed of the manifestation.

Supplies: Weaving; chocolate chips; pennies.

- Find the ideal spot for your weaving.

- Push it into the ground so it's solidly implanted.

- Scatter and bury chocolate chips and pennies throughout the area, as well. These are gifts of money and food for the local devas or earth spirits. You're asking them for help, so it's proper to give them a gift.

- Leave, and let it go (i.e., put it out of your mind so it can do its work).

Exercise 19

Making Love to Your Soulmate

No book of exercises for attracting your soulmate is complete without evoking the most intimate and ecstatic connection between you— that of making love. For in doing so, you are allowing your physical body to experience what it's like to have your soulmate touch you at the very core of your desire. After all, any relationship that doesn't involve all parts of your Self is ultimately unfulfilling. Love needs to be embraced at every level.

When you make love to your soulmate, you do it both on the physical plane and in your mind, when you take a journey into your inner world. Let's start there first.

Simply close your eyes and imagine meeting your soulmate in a special place, perhaps the one you have been to before or maybe some place different, somewhere that conveys intimacy to you—in a garden, in a secluded arbor, in your bedroom or another bedroom. That's where you two can be together in all your combined emotional, physical, and spiritual glory.

Since it's all in your mind, the only censor is yourself, and any limitations are imposed by you alone. You can go hog wild, if you want, acting out every kind of fantasy that your imagination allows, or be as simple and pure as you feel. Indulge yourself.

Now, mentally creating a love situation between you two can be a delightful and exhilarating intellectual exercise. And daydreams are certainly enjoyable. But the impact and the potency become more tangible when you add a physical dimension, when your physical body can experience what your mind is imagining. That means experiencing physical pleasure.

When you call in your soulmate's essence and pleasure yourself, you actually experience its erotic intensity in all layers and cells of your body. That adds an incredible emotional resonance to your own sexual enjoyment, and heightens your personal ecstasy.

Not only is it a completely enjoyable fantasy, but it serves as a kind of preparation so that when you two actually get together, you'll already have created that rhythm of intimacy between you. And, believe me, your bodies will recognize each other!

Let's carry this process one step further, into your outer-world relationship. This inner joining creates a sensual response in the outer world. People who have often self-pleasured with their soulmate's essence report that they feel more desirable as a person. And that means they carry themselves differently. They feel that they are worthy of being loved.

Making physical love with a lover becomes much more intense and erotic. (After all, you're not expected to be celibate while you're waiting.) That's because you are not just sharing with the person you're with; you're sharing with the person you're not with (yet), over the air waves, on the etheric and spiritual planes. Their energy really does mingle with yours. Each time you have intimacy with any physical partner, your soulmate experiences it as well because your body is remembering the enjoyment it has whenever you do this exercise.

Sex generates powerful kundalini (creative/libido) energy; as you become more engaged with your partner, the kundalini rises. Bringing your soulmate into this equation enhances the intensity of your experience and also strengthens the bond between you two. This is a way you can meet them on a most physical and intimate level. With your eyes closed, you can pretend it's your soulmate stroking you, caressing you, kissing your body, letting their tongue run around your ear, reaching climax.

This is the essence of a spiritual joining using sex. Every part of you sings. Your lovemaking becomes marvelously potent. You experience the whole sexual act on a physical, emotional, and spiritual level.

But before I continue, I need to bring up a very important caution: If you are in a committed partnership or marriage, why are you doing this process?

Of all the exercises in the book, this one can cause an enormous reaction in your life because it is so intimate and potent. Doing this kind of soulmate work may disrupt your current relationship. I don't want to be responsible for a marriage breakup. Nor do I advocate destroying your present relationship in order to meet your soulmate.

You need to ask yourself these very important questions: What is it about my present relationship that is making me look elsewhere? What happens if I do all this work religiously, and my soulmate shows up? What then? You need to consider and address these concerns when the time is right, preferably before something happens.

Are you really committed to that relationship? Or are you content to make a connection with your soulmate's energy, and do nothing more? I know some people who have made just that decision; they have found that their sex life with their present partner is much more intense because of that extra, added juice. And they intend to do nothing more. They're content with the way things are now—and their soulmate, much as they would like to know them, would complicate the picture (this is particularly true if there are children involved).

It's a matter for your own conscience and your own highest wisdom. Aside from that caveat, if you are not in a meaningful partnership, this process can create an enormous erotic magnetism in you whenever you do it.

I have mentioned calling on your soulmate in your dreams before. After you have done this exercise of sexual union, invite your soulmate to have sex with you on the astral plane, in dream land. This is an exciting experience.

In this exercise I'm going to focus on your mental fantasy, not the physical one; you can figure that out by yourself.

Supplies: Anything that gives you pleasure: Love oil, love incense, a vibrator, sexy magazines or videos (the list is endless); a pillow or two. Put on some music that invites intimacy, either romantic or exciting.

Duration: As long as you want.

- Do the Grounding, Energy Clean-out, and Retrieving Your Energy exercises (page 38).

- Get yourself in a romantic mood, including music, soft candlelight, scented bath, and so on. Get comfortable in whatever place feels the most inviting (after all, your physical surroundings add to your pleasure).

- Close your eyes and imagine yourself going out into a place that feels good to you—a bedroom, a natural setting, et cetera.

- Invite your soulmate essence to come and join you in this place. Imagine them coming across the field, or down the sands, or through the door toward you. Open your arms to welcome them. (You can actually move your arms in a welcoming gesture.)

- Greet each other as passionately as you would wish. Feel their energy coming around you, and yours around them, so you two are merged together.

- Do what you want to do with each other, holding, touching, stroking, kissing, loving. As you run your hands across your body, across your chest and face and groin, touching all of those places on your body that are erotic zones for you, imagine it's their hands that are stroking you. You may want to hug or stroke the pillow (it provides the sensation of holding something firm, like your soulmate's torso).

- Get as involved as you wish to. If you want to make this physical, pleasure yourself while you are having the mental experience. That's why indulging in your sexual fantasies can be so delightful. Naturally, your pleasure is limited only by your own imagination and desire.

- When you're finished, thank your soulmate for coming in the most loving and erotic way.

- Before you leave them, invite them to come into your dreams. Let them be a part of yours on the astral plane. You may or may not remember these encounters, at first, but if you make that the last thought before going to sleep—that you two will meet in your dreams, and remember it—you are likely to find them happening more often.

Invoking a Goddess

You have called on your angels for assistance. Now it's time to call on another divine being: A goddess. Yes, such beings do exist. When you call on a goddess (or a god), you are reaching back to the ancient god forms. Although they are no longer universally worshiped, these divine beings still retain their power and wisdom, and are still available for you to call on.

In our Western culture, most of us are used to calling on Mother Mary, or Jesus Christ, or saints (if you're Catholic) to provide us with what we desire. Generally, they are all-purpose helpers (although particular saints may work for certain causes). These are latter-day "gods."

By calling on a goddess (or a god), you are actually invoking their presence to listen to your prayer and intercede in some way to create a desired result in your life. In effect, you can hand over the responsibility for manifestation to them, letting them handle the details. All you do is just keep praying and invoking until it occurs.

Before you invoke these divine beings, you need to consider which goddess or god that you want to ask for help. Mythology books will give details on the attributes and aspects of particular gods and goddesses. In this case, since you are looking to attract your soulmate into your life, it's not unreasonable that you would want to call in a goddess of love. You can also broaden the scope to include fecundity, female power, and strength. Choose a goddess whose qualities help you in manifesting your soulmate relationship. There are love goddesses from all kinds of cultures. Some are passionate or turbulent; others have qualities that are more sedate or compassionate. Yet all are committed to love and lovers, and they can use their power to help you attract your soulmate.

The love goddess that is most familiar to us is Aphrodite (Venus). Her son is Amor (Eros), the god of love (but he's subordinate to the far more potent goddess). Aphrodite is known for her active and capricious love life, loving passionately but not necessarily wisely. Her love is wrapped up in sexual passion.

Since Aphrodite is known to be a fickle goddess, you can invoke her help in calling in a lover; but with her help you may not necessarily receive the *right* lover. She definitely will create a love relationship for you, but it may not be your soulmate. Cupid's arrows have been known to misconnect. Is this the kind of divinity you want to have help you?

Love goddesses generally respond to prayers from you to manifest your true love. After all, that's what pleases them most—bringing love into people's lives. When you invoke them, you have to be specific about what you're looking for; otherwise, they'll give you whatever they find.

What about gods? Love gods are rare or are subsumed under the goddesses. Gods are generally celebrated for their wisdom, power, and warlike prowess, whereas love is the province of goddesses. In reality, the gender of the goddess or god doesn't matter; what's important is whether your prayers are being heard and acted upon. You may decide to invoke both a god and a goddess; it works best if they come from the same culture. However, I think it's best to focus on only one goddess. Don't scatter your energy around.

Love goddesses you might want to call on include the following (but there are more I haven't listed):

- Aphrodite (Greek), Venus (Roman)

- Freya (Norse)—beauty, love

- Hathor (Egyptian)—love, beauty

- Ishtar (Sumerian), Inanna (Babylonian)—love goddess

- Isis (Egyptian)—wisdom, love, strength, power

- Kuan-Yin (Chinese)—compassion, grace, mercy

- Lakshmi (Indian)—pleasure, beauty, wealth

- Oshun (Africa)—love, fertility

Get a mythology book out of the library or look up goddesses on the Internet, and read up on them. This will help you get a sense of what goddess might feel right to you. Use your own intuition to decide which one to call on.

Once you've made your choice, get a picture of her. That will be essential when doing your goddess invocation. Photocopy it out of a book if that's the only way to obtain it (but don't wreck the book). Even better, browse the Internet. There are many websites devoted to these ancient beings with wonderful goddess images that you can download.

If you'd prefer to have a statue or something three-dimensional, check out your local metaphysical or New Age store for goddess statues. There is a vast range of religious figures available nowadays, and the list is expanding all the time. You can also check the web for on-line dealers.

Now that you have chosen your goddess and procured a symbol or picture of her, you can prepare for your invocation. You want to make this ritual as potent as possible. That means not only using your intent but also the energies that are available to you from the larger cosmic forces. Here are some energies you can tap to enhance your ritual.

- Do your ritual on Friday. This is the day assigned to Venus/Aphrodite, who is, of course, the goddess of love. After all, this is what this work is all about—finding your special love.

- The best time for the ritual is at the first hour of the day or night, which means at dawn or dusk. There is more power at those times ("the turning of the day") than later on. You can check your newspaper for the official times of dawn and dusk.

- Do your ritual during the waxing moon, not the waning moon. As the moon gets full (waxes), it is in its attraction mode (i.e., what you want comes to you), while its waning phase means letting go. You want love to come to you, not go away. If you're not sure about what stage the moon is in, get a calendar that shows the moon phases.

Be sure that your soulmate is with you during this ritual. That lets the goddess know what particular energies she should be searching for. After doing all this work, you don't want the goddess to make a mistake and give you someone who's not your soulmate!

When you invoke the goddess and ask for her help, you are passing the request over to her to manifest. It's like taking your burden and handing it on to the goddess. That's why it's a good idea to ask her to give you a particular sign of acknowledgment that she has heard your plea.

You may occasionally sense from the goddess what sign she will give you. Flowers are a common sign (like a rose), or a certain message. Quite often you receive them, not from friends, but from strangers that come into your life just for a moment, long enough to pass them on. Even if you doubt you will get it, ask anyway. I guarantee you that these requests get fulfilled, sometimes in strange ways.

Fern prayed for a boon from Kuan-Yin, and asked for a rose. The next day she got a picture with roses all over them. She took that as a sign that her prayer was answered, and indeed it was.

Maryanne called on Isis to bring her a lover, and got the image of a gardenia as her sign. The next day, her part-time lover gave her a white rose, which she accepted as close enough to a gardenia (it was white and smelled good). Soon afterward, their whole relationship transformed into exactly what she wanted.

Supplies: Pink altar cloth; picture or statue of goddess; pink and red candles; flowering plant (preferably the one from exercise 17, otherwise, a plant with pink flowers); patchouli or jasmine incense; love oil.

Duration: 30–45 minutes.

- Do the Grounding, Energy Clean-out, and Retrieving Your Energy exercises (page 38).

- Prepare a space on your altar. If you don't have one, use a shelf or table. You will be sitting or standing in front of it. Remove everything. Cover the altar with the pink altar cloth, and arrange the following on it: a picture or statue of the goddess, a red candle on the left side, a pink candle on the right; the flowering plant on the left, and the incense on the right.

- Light the candles.

- Light the incense and pass it across the altar and where you're standing or sitting to purify the area and raise it to the vibration of love.

- Call in your soulmate's essence to stand or sit beside you. They, too, need to participate in this invocation. Pretend that they're beside you, no matter what you do (or don't) feel.

- Anoint your wrists, ankles, brow, and heart with the love oil and say, "As I anoint myself with this oil, I open myself to the love between my soulmate and me. My heart is filled with our love. I vibrate to the energy of our love. I feel it within me and around me."

- Raising your hands, palms out in supplication, call on your chosen goddess. Put your heart and soul in it. These are my words, but you may change them or add your own words, of course. For this exercise, I chose Isis. When you say these words, use the name of your goddess.

"O (Isis), I call on you to listen to my prayer. I ask you to come to me now." Repeat this invocation once more.

"My soulmate is here beside me. We stand before you, (Isis), my soulmate and I, calling on your divine Will and divine Grace. Grant my prayer to bring my soulmate and me together in physical form so that we may be in a love relationship—and only if it is in alignment with our higher good. [This is *very important*. You don't want to create a relationship that is not right for either of you.] Help me, (Isis), I pray."

- You may repeat these words or add your own.

- Holding the plant in your hands, imagine your soulmate's hands around yours. Say, "I call on you, (Isis), to help me create a relationship with my soulmate that will grow and flower like this plant."

- Now pray silently, asking the goddess for her help. Ask your soulmate to join in. This lets the goddess tune into your combined energies. After all, you want her to find that particular energy, not just anyone.

- If you have a good erotic fantasy, this is a good time to indulge in it. Sexual excitement brings up a lot of kundalini energy. Goddesses (love goddesses, in particular) respond to that energy. If you want them to bring you your true love, she wants to know that you're seriously committed to your cause.

- Ask the goddess for a sign that she has heard your prayer and is working on it. Relax your mind to tune into any images. If you don't get anything, you might ask that she send you something in particular, like a flower or, more specifically, a rose.

- When you're done, douse the incense but let the candles burn out on their own. Leave the altar intact as long as possible. This may not be practical, depending on your living situation, but if you can see the goddess' image daily, it's a reminder to pray to her to keep working on your request.

Exercise 21

Attraction Ritual

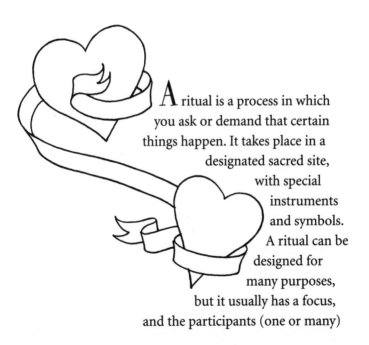

A ritual is a process in which you ask or demand that certain things happen. It takes place in a designated sacred site, with special instruments and symbols. A ritual can be designed for many purposes, but it usually has a focus, and the participants (one or many)

have a particular goal in mind. A familiar and beautifully ornate ritual is the Catholic mass: It takes place at a specific time, with special instruments, in a special, consecrated area, and with a particular ceremony and a specific goal.

There are many ways to do rituals. In this ritual, you will focus your will toward the goal of bringing your soulmate to you. It requires several ceremonial objects:

- A bell, to move you from ordinary time and space into this special altered space

- A sword or dagger for banishing energies

- A wand to call in divine energies; your wand can be something as simple as a twig 12–18 inches long, one of those crystal wands you can buy at the store, or a plastic wand with floating stars in it—whatever feels right to you

- A chalice for sacred liquid—you're going to be drinking it, so don't put in too much

- Incense

- Pink and red candles

- Pink altar cloth

- Pink paper

- Red pen

If you already have some of these objects as part of your spiritual practice, you may use them. Don't use objects from your everyday life. You want items that are designated for this purpose. (If you are not sure about all this, there are a number of books that describe magical rituals in great detail.) When in doubt, buy them new (you want them to have neutral energy).

You also need a sigil (a special love sign) to put on the wall behind your altar (see diagram at right) to serve as your focus.

The clothing you wear is important. You may wear white, black, or the appropriate color for the purpose. In this case, red would be the desired color.

Do this ritual on Friday, the day of Venus, or Monday, the moon day, the day of emotion, and during the two weeks of the waxing moon. (You can get even more elaborate in your times, but these conditions are enough.)

Keep in mind that you are not looking to attract just any person. You are attracting your soulmate, your special lover—a specific energy. The whole ritual is focused on magnetizing the person to you. As usual, you will be calling in your Higher Self, angels, and any other higher beings to assist and guide you. So if you don't do the ritual "perfectly," it won't ruin the effect. Missed or fumbled steps will not matter—rituals work because of focus and intent.

Once you have completed the ritual, you need to let it go, just like you did with the calling (exercise 18). The more you keep thinking about it afterward, the more you hold on to its energy, and it can't do its job of attracting your soulmate. It's like holding on to your spouse's hand when they're trying to go to work. They can't earn money at your doorstep. They have to leave.

Supplies: See list, page 222.

Duration: 30–45 minutes. Once you begin the ritual, don't interrupt it. That really disrupts the energy. So make sure you have privacy.

- Do the Grounding, Energy Clean-out, and Retrieving Your Energy exercises (page 38). It is often recommended that you fast for a day beforehand and do meditation for at least one hour in advance. Make your own decision about that. The more you focus, the stronger your ritual will be.

- Dress yourself in the appropriate clothing.

- Draw your sigil on pink paper with the red pen and stick it on the wall.

- Arrange your altar as you did for exercise 20. Put your plant (from exercise 17) on the altar just below the sigil, as well as any other objects you've made (doll, shield, collage, talisman).

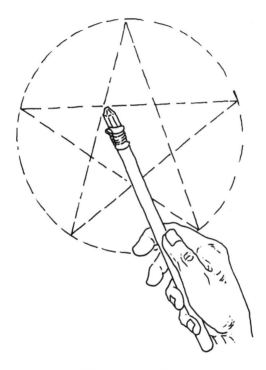

Using your wand, inscribe a
pentagram in the air.

- Put on music that enhances your love.

- Ring your bell in each of the four directions to
  define the sacred space; this moves you from
  everyday reality to a sacred reality.

- Use your dagger to banish all unwanted energies
  in the four directions. Turn to the east first.
  Draw a pentagram in the air, and say, "I send all
  unwanted energies back to the east." Repeat
  those words in the other directions (substituting
  south, west, and north).

- Facing each direction, call in the appropriate element for the direction: east is air; south is fire;
  west is water; north is earth. Using your wand,
  inscribe a pentagram in the air; as you do, say,
  "I call in the element of (insert element here)
  to assist me in my ritual."

- Call in your Higher Self and other higher beings
  to assist you in this attraction ritual. Ask them to
  help you bring your soulmate to you, if it is in
  the highest good for both of you.

- Anoint yourself with the love oil. Put it on your feet, brow, heart, and palms, and say, "I am open to my soulmate's love."

- Burn the love (or other) incense.

- Say the following aloud: "I call in my soulmate's energy. I call them to me. I ask them to be with me, to share their essence with me. I call on the wind to bring them to me." Pause to let it happen.

- "I call on my soulmate energy through the fire. Let it burn hot and strong. And anything that's in the way gets burned up, so that the essence of my soulmate, which is strong and powerful, can be here with me." Pause.

- "I call on my soulmate to be brought here with the water, which washes away anything in the way of my soulmate. I embrace my soulmate through the waters that move my soulmate to me, as the waters of our love flow through us. We are strong, powerful, and we are as one." Pause.

- "I call on my soulmate to feel the power, strength, and solidity of earth, so our love will last as long as we want. I call on my soulmate to stand with me, grounded and solid, in our life together." Pause to imagine your soulmate coming toward you, hands outstretched.

- "I ask for the blessings of the angels and (name the divine beings you have summoned). Share your essence with my soulmate and me. Surround us with love." Pause.

- "I call upon my soulmate to embrace me, to fill me, to complete me." Feel your soulmate's energy beside, around, and in you.

- Hold up the chalice and face the sigil. Say, "I ask that this chalice be filled with the essence of love between me and my soulmate." Drink it all.

- Pick up one of your talismans. Holding it, visualize you and your soulmate being together. Say, "With this (name the object), I summon my

soulmate to my side." Then you can repeat
the process with each of the objects. The more
you concentrate and focus, the stronger the
connection.

- Anoint the sigil with the love oil. Say, "Let my
  soulmate come to me across time and space."

- This is the point where some people may want to
  self-pleasure, to heighten the enjoyment and
  intensity of the ritual, and to do it with the sense
  of your soulmate being with you. Although this
  is not a sex-oriented ritual, the reason sex magic
  is so popular is that it stimulates the kundalini
  energy so you can use it to direct your will. Since
  this is your ritual, you have that option.

- Finally, it is time to complete the ritual. Thank
  the divine beings for coming and invite them to
  leave. Thank your soulmate and send them back.

- Send back the directional energies using the wand to inscribe the pentagram. "I send back the powers of (air, fire, water, earth)."

- Use the dagger or sword to banish all the energies that have accumulated. Facing each direction, say, "I send back all unwanted energies to the (east, south, west, north)."

- Ring your bell to end the ritual.

- Blow out the candles. Break them, and throw them away.

- Put everything away, including the sigil.

- Let the ritual go (i.e., put it out of your mind so it can do its work).

Conclusion

Now that you've completed the exercises in this book, maybe you'd like to compare yourself now to how you were before you started—your attitudes and feelings about yourself, others, and your soulmate. Are you still the same old person, or can you detect clear differences in yourself? Let's find out. Very often it's hard for us to see the changes we've gone through because they're so subtle, but others can see them, and so can we once we have them in black and white.

At the beginning, I asked you to fill out a checklist on yourself. Before you pull out that first list, create another checklist. Then compare them to see how you've changed. Here's the list again, on page 235.

Now compare the lists. If you discover some items on the old list you'd like to include on the new list, be sure to add them.

First, notice which items show up on both lists. Let's examine them carefully. Do you feel the same resonance or intensity about them as you did before? Let's track that. Write down a plus (+) or a minus (-) beside the item on the new checklist to indicate what kind of improvement has occurred.

For example, you might have listed "depressed"; now that becomes "pretty happy." That's a plus. "Scared" in the first list has turned to "open and welcoming." That rates a plus. Or "infrequently short-tempered" on the first list has

The Snapshot Form

Likes, in general (about anything)	Dislikes, in general (about anything)
Personal qualities you like	Personal qualities you dislike
Characteristics (what makes you different from everyone else in the world)	What the ideal you would look and be like
Fears (personal and global)	Ideal mate
Hopes and dreams (personal and for others)	Ideal world (business and home)
Spiritual beliefs	What is important to you

become "often short-tempered." Is that a minus change or not? (Becoming more testy may be indicative of not being as compliant as you were, which is a good thing.)

Do that for every quality that appears on both lists.

Next, cross off, on your old list, whatever items didn't make the new list.

Study the new list. That gives you a picture of yourself now. You can see how far you've progressed in your own development, and how much more open and accepting you are of someone new in your life.

Remember, no matter what happens with your soulmate, this is your transformation. I hope you have enjoyed your journey of discovery, and that all your prayers and dreams have been fulfilled. It's wonderful when things work out well.

If you'd like to share your journey, your experiences, any modifications you've made in the exercises, and your results with me, please do so. You can e-mail me at arians@rocketmail.com. I'd love to hear from you.

Resource List

I have set up this resource list by category and by chapter. That means you can look up vendors of particular items. Or you can consult the list of items required for certain chapters. (Some chapters do not require any specific items.)

Some of these items are available anywhere, but many need to come from a specialty store. Below is a limited listing of places where you can obtain particular kinds of items referred to in this book. Many of them are wholesalers, not retailers. There is a reason for this. I have found that in the metaphysical community, retailers come and go, unfortunately; wholesalers tend to have a longer survival rate.

Besides, if you contact the wholesaler, they will gladly tell you where in your area of the world you can buy their products. Most of them have either websites, e-mail, or 800 numbers for ease of contact. Others are both retailer and wholesaler, particularly those who are on the Internet—and more are coming on every day.

The Internet has become a godsend (so to speak) if you want specific items. All you have to do is search for your item, and you'll find quite a selection. Luckily, many of the people that I have listed here are quickly building websites, though some don't even have computers.

I contacted all of these people; some of them supplied me with their products, but most provided their catalogs. They were all scanned for any items that would fit the theme of this book, that of enhancing your connection with your soulmate. I have not included prices because those change at a moment's notice, and different retailers may choose to have their own prices.

I have listed them alphabetically and by category. I must remind you that these are just a few of the very many different and wonderful companies making the various products that I talk about in the book.

Angels

These I didn't make a list for. There are just so many stores that carry angels, from card stores and department stores to knickknack stores and a ton of Internet sites. There are whole websites devoted to listing angel websites! There are lots of statues, pictures, plaques, pins, etc., available in every shape, size, color, and dimension.

Aromatherapy Oils and Flower Essences

Love oil is called for in several activities, or some variation thereof. The following companies have a variety of love oils that would serve excellently.

DRAGONMARSH
3737 6th St.
Riverside, CA 92501
Phone: (909) 276-1116
e-mail: store@dragonmarsh.com
www.dragonmarsh.com

Love oils, along with other magical and spiritual oils.

HEART OF THE GODDESS
P.O. Box 446
Sedona, AZ 86339
Phone: (541) 201-0097
e-mail: mcordeo@yahoo.com

> Channeled, divinely-inspired essential oil blends for meditation, ceremony, and self-attunement, including Angel Blessings, Love's Promise, Ascension Blends, Goddess Blends, and Aphrodite. These oils take love into high spiritual connection and alignment, as well as just plain enjoyment.

STARMEN UNLIMITED
P.O. Box 698
Kilauea, HI 96754
Phone: (808) 828-1946
Fax: (808) 808-1329
e-mail: starman@aloha.net

> Kauai flower and gem essences for Divine Love, Erotic Lovemaking, Deep Emotional Release, Love Essence, Male and Female Synergy, Sexual Clarity, Relationships, and Spirit Connection.

TERRY & CO.
300D West Robles Ave.
Santa Rosa, CA 95407
Phone: (707) 586-3019
Fax: (707) 586-3235
e-mail: FragranceGoddess@juno.com

> Egyptian botanical fragrances, including Hathor Rising, Dreams of Isis, Cleopatra's Secret, and Nefertiti.

You might also want to concoct something on your own. I recommend highly the book *Magical Aromatherapy* by Scott Cunningham (Llewellyn, 1989), which describes every kind of ingredients for making love oils that you can mix and match according to your own desires and intuition—in which case, you should invite in your soulmate essence to help you create your "special love oil" that is attuned to your combined love vibration.

Candles

ANGELIC MERCANTILE
P.O. Box 21824
Eugene, OR 97402
Phone: (800) 344-8002
Fax: (541) 689-9330

> Gem Crystal Candles, containing actual crystals and aromatherapy oils: Love, Opening the Heart, Attunement, Creative Inspiration, Sweet Surrender, Emotional Balance, Venus Rising, etc. Also Essence Aromatherapy candles.

SWEET SPIRIT CANDLES
916 S. 3rd Street
Renton, WA 98055
Phone: (888) 871-9001
e-mail: More_Info@sweetspiritcandles.com
www.sweetspiritcandles.com

Sacred candles combining crystals, colors, and scents for love and relationships: Attracting Happy Relationships, Attracting Soulmates, Attracting True Love, Deep Romantic Love, Grounding Sexual Energy, Jungle Love, Mending Relationships, Passionate Love, Seduction, Timeless Love, etc.

TERRY & CO.
(see previous citation)

Ritual Illuminates "for the magic of the moment," including Unconditional Love, Pleasure, Passion, Transcendence, and Mystery.

Crystals

Let your Higher Self make the choice of what crystals are best for you. Hold them in your hand and put them next to your forehead or along your body to see if they resonate with you. Here are two companies that are willing to sell direct, although I personally prefer to hold them to sense which crystals are "right."

CRYSTAL CLEAR
P.O. Box 185
Greenbrier, AR 72058
e-mail: swhite@cyberback.com

Crystals to enhance your life, encourage a meeting with your soulmate, help you understand your purpose in life, and heal yourself emotionally or physically to make yourself whole for the relationship you deserve.

HEAVEN AND EARTH
RR 1, Box 25
Marshfield, VT 05658
Phone: (800) 942-9423
Fax: (802) 426-3441

All kinds of crystals, pendants, and jewelry using high-vibration crystals, minerals, and gems.

You can also find crystals at New Age stores, rock shops, and on the Internet. Some of the ones on the Internet give pictures.

Goddesses

ANCIENT CIRCLES/OPEN CIRCLE
1750 East Hill Rd
Willits, CA 95490
Phone: (800) 726-8032
Fax: (707) 459-0261
e-mail: ancient@pacific.net
www.ancientcircles.com

Celtic focussed; ritual/goddess clothing, and symbols.

ANCIENT TREASURES
P.O. Box 765
Woodland Hills, CA 91365
Phone: (800) 760-0032
Fax: (818) 706-3704

> Their color catalog is quite luscious. They have a lot of Egyptian goddess statues and plaques, a number of seated Buddhas, Kuan-Yins, and archangel plaques.

JBL STATUES
Box 163
Crozet, VA 22932-0163
Phone: (800) 290-6203 or (804) 823-1515
e-mail: jblstatue@jblstatue.com
www.jblstatue.com

> They have a vast catalog of goddess statues. Their on-line catalog not only gives you the pictures, but the historical perspective.

MISSION STUDIOS
℅ Light Stones
5375 Western Ave. #2
Boulder, CO 80301
Phone: (800) 82-PEACE

> All kinds of divine and religious figures: Angels, East Indian gods and goddesses like Lakshmi, Parvati, Kuan-Yin, Mother Mary, Jesus, Buddha, and the Mother Goddess. The statues are quite small (usually 2–3" high), off-white resin, and very detailed.

NATALIE LYNN COMPANY
925 Walnut Street
Traverse City, MI 49686
Phone: (800) 497-4108
e-mail: nlynn@gtii.com
www.traverse.net/natalielynn
Wholesale and retail

> Clay goddess talisman to draw her energies to you, with appropriate symbols.

Incense

Nag Champa is an East Indian incense; the most popular is that devised by Sai Baba, the Indian teacher and guru. You can obtain it at most metaphysical stores.

AARON ANDERSEN, INC.
4915-H High Point Rd.
Greensboro, NC 27407
Phone: (336) 854-8599
Fax: (336) 854-1065
e-mail: info@aaolc.com

EYE OF THE DAY
4850 Sterling Dr.
Boulder, CO 80301
www.eyeoftheday.com
e-mail: eyeoftheday@msn.com

This is a wholesaler and representative for many companies. They had been just selling wholesale, but their website is set up to deal with the public. They have a vast number of items.

ISHTAROMATICS
1122 E. Pike St., Suite 921
Seattle, WA 98122
Phone: (206) 464-8369
www.ishtaromatics.com

Native American incenses include sweetgrass, cedar, copal, and sage. You can obtain these at many New Age stores, and many sites on the web.

There are also specialty incenses that focus on particular situations, such as making love, calling your lover to you, or getting yourself into the mood to invite your lover.

AIRS INTERNATIONAL
P.O. Box 458
Capitola, CA 95010-0458
www.airsworld.com

They make wonderful incenses, and there are several focused directly on relationships: Rain Musk, Angel Dreams, Hearts of Rose, and Kashmir.

NATALIE LYNN COMPANY
(see previous citation)

> Turtle Moon Premium Stick Incense: Passion scent—to attract and enhance love and passion.

Music

There are so many varieties of music these days, I would recommend just going to a music store and listening to their selections. Buy what appeals to you.

The kind of music you'll want for a particular activity is directly connected to what kind of mood you want to evoke. If you want to be passionate, you want something that has life to it, and joy and passion. Ravel's "Bolero" comes to mind, as well as Brazilian music. There is something truly passionate and sensuous about the Brazilian beat. And nothing beats tango music for setting the blood to boil!

If you want to create an intimate moment, more sinuous, complex music might be of interest, like Spanish, Middle Eastern, or Celtic music. And of course, there is a full range of variety in and among these three categories.

If you are into meditation, some quiet New Age-type of music would be perfect. There's a temptation to make suggestions, but I have to say that what I like might well be different from what appeals to you.

There is Native American flute music (Douglas Spotted Horse, Carlos Nakai, and others), which might be very useful when doing the shield or weaving a calling exercises.

There is also a program called *Echoes* on National Public Radio, which is completely New Age music. Check with your local NPR station when or if they run the program. National Public Radio publishes a playlist of their selections at www.echoes.org.

Another really wonderful program is *Hearts of Space*, which is also on NPR, usually on Sunday nights. They too have a playlist, which you can find at www.heartsofspace.com. Both *Echoes* and *Hearts of Space* also provide an opportunity for you to listen to previous programs, which will give you a taste of what kind of music you might like. They also have compilations from various artists on a theme, which are quite pleasant. I have several of them.

When I mention meditation music, I personally enjoy something very quiet and soothing, like anything by Stephen Halprin, Georgia Kelly, John Serrie, Jon Mark, and Iasos. But there are many, many more artists who put out wonderful music.

Ritual Accoutrements

These are tools for ritual work, for helping you focus your will and intent on your work. Some of these are very specific to your work. Others add to the ambience of what you want to create.

ANCIENT CIRCLES/OPEN CIRCLE
(see previous citation)

> Celtic designs; ritual/goddess clothing; and a lot of ritual talismans.

CRYSTAL MIST
262 Post Rd.
Guffey, CO 80820
Phone: (800) 279-7647
e-mail: melnjo@aol.com

> Carved glass goblets, pentagrams, and other ritual items, as well as goddess and wiccan imagery.

NANCY B. WATSON'S POTIONS
59 Park Terrace
Mill Valley, CA 94941
Phone: (800) 380-1080
Fax: (415) 383-4227

> Really useful powders and waters for all kinds of magical work. Includes goddess potions, love and relationship enhancing powders, love water, et cetera.

NATALIE LYNN COMPANY
(see previous citation)

> Herbs, candles, and love-wishing powder.

Sexual Enhancement Items

Well, this is a loaded area. You can do and find all kinds of items to enhance your enjoyment of sex with your lover. Some of this may be private; others may be with your lover. Yes, there are all kinds of sex sites on the web, and sex shops; but in this book we're not talking about sex, we're talking about romance and love.

ISHTAROMATICS
(see previous citation)

> Kama Sutra products—exactly what you want for a sensual experience with your lover. Such products include the

Earthly Delight Gift Drum, where myriad pleasures await the curious, to be discovered as romance unfolds with Oil of Love, Pleasure Balm, Honey Dust, and Honey Almond Massage Cream. They have other creamy delights as well.

If you want to pleasure yourself, or have your partner pleasure you, I would suggest going to a store like Good Vibrations (www.goodvibes.com) for all kinds of wonderful sex toys. These are not prurient, but enjoyable.

Talismans

NATALIE LYNN COMPANY
(see previous citation)

Cinnamon heart talisman with appropriate traditional symbols.

EYE OF THE DAY
(see previous citation)

They have a number of items—statuettes, images, pictures—that would work well as talismans.

ANCIENT CIRCLES/OPEN CIRCLE
(see previous citation)

Celtic designs; ritual/goddess clothing, a lot of ritual talismans.

Tapes

I put out my own tapes of some of the exercises in this book; to order, contact me at arians@rocketmail.com

- Meeting Your Soulmate (exercise 1)
- Who You Attract (exercise 4)

Special 21 Ways Kits

Candle Burning Kit (exercise 12)

Includes pink, red, black and white candles, love incense, love oil, decorative hearts, and a copy of the exercise. These candles are specially prepared in advance with a special love vibration ritual, so that you will be getting an extra focus of energy when you use them.

The Doll Kit (exercise 13)

Includes a small (7") cloth doll form (similar to page 154), paper hearts, pink and red ribbons, and felt tip pen. With this doll you can create your own soulmate focus.

The Talisman Kit (exercise 16)

Includes rose quartz heart, love incense, love oil, red and pink paper, heart-shaped paper, small colored pouch. These objects have been energetically cleansed so that you will receive a talisman that is ready for your work.

To order kits or for more information, visit my website:
www.geocities.com/arians.rm.

Chapters That Require Specific Items

Resources:

Altar supplies: God/dess statutes, pictures, crystals, angel cards, incense, candles.

Exercise 3, Inviting Your Soulmate Into Your Life:

Patchouli or jasmine incense, love incense.

Exercise 7, Dreaming Your Soulmate into Reality:

Love oil, sage, patchouli, jasmine incense, love incense.

Exercise 9, The Beacon:

Sweet grass or Nag Champa incense.

Exercise 11, Angels and the Cosmic Cord:

Angel images.

Exercise 12, Candle Burning:

Candles—pink, white, black.

Exercise 13, The Doll:

Nag Champa incense; dolls from toy or party store; crayons; magic markers; colored ribbons (most of this comes from toy stores or fabric/craft stores).

Exercise 15, The Shield:

Sweet grass, copal, and sage incense; decorative items.

Exercise 16, The Talisman:

Talisman (angel picture or figure, love object, picture or figure); love incense; love oil; candle.

Exercise 17, The Flowering Plant:

Patchouli or jasmine incense; love incense; mylar confetti; candle.

Exercise 18, Weaving a Calling:

Copal, sage, or sweetgrass incense; native flute music.

Exercise 19, Making Love to Your Soulmate:

Candles; romantic or passionate music; love oil; love incense.

Exercise 20, Invoking a Goddess:

Goddess picture, object, plaque, or statue; love oil; love, patchouli, or jasmine incense; pink and red candles.

Exercise 21, Attraction Ritual:

Bell; dagger; wand; chalice; incense; candles; love oil; love, patchouli, or jasmine incense.